Continuing the Search
for Religious Freedom

Fifty Years after Vatican II's
Dignitatis Humanae

Continuing the Search for Religious Freedom

Fifty Years after Vatican II's

Dignitatis Humanae

Edited by

Dennis J. Billy, C.Ss.R.

LEONINE PUBLISHERS
PHOENIX, ARIZONA

NIHIL OBSTAT

Rev. Robert A. Pesarchick
Censor Librorum
Philadelphiae, 10-28-2015

IMPRIMATUR

✠ Most Rev. Charles J. Chaput, OFM Cap.
Archiepiscopus Philadelphiensis
Philadelphiae, 10-30-2015

Published by Leonine Publishers LLC
Phoenix, Arizona
USA

ISBN-13: 978-1-942190-24-0

Library of Congress Control Number: 2016930480

Printed in the United States of America
10 9 8 7 6 5 4 3 2 1

Visit us online at www.leoninepublishers.com
For more information: info@leoninepublishers.com

For all

who thirst for

religious freedom

This Vatican Council declares that the human person has a right to religious freedom. This freedom means that all men are to be immune from coercion on the part of individuals or of social groups and of any human power, in such wise that no one is to be forced to act in a manner contrary to his own beliefs, whether privately or publicly, whether alone or in association with others, within due limits.

The council further declares that the right to religious freedom has its foundation in the very dignity of the human person as this dignity is known through the revealed word of God and by reason itself. This right of the human person to religious freedom is to be recognized in the constitutional law whereby society is governed and thus it is to become a civil right.

Dignitatis Humanae, no. 2

Contents

Acknowledgments

Unless otherwise stated, all quotations from Sacred Scripture come from the *New American Bible*, available on the Vatican website at http://www.vatican.va/archive/ENG0839/_INDEX.HTM.

Unless otherwise stated, all quotations from Catholic magisterial documents come from the Vatican website at http://www.vatican.va/phome_en.htm.

The "Prayer for the Protection of Religious Liberty" is copyrighted by the United States Conference of Catholic Bishops and used with permission.

Foreword

During the spring semester of the 2014–2015 academic year, St. Charles Borromeo Seminary of the Archdiocese of Philadelphia sponsored a lecture series, under the auspices of the John Cardinal Krol Chair of Moral Theology, entitled "Continuing the Search for Religious Freedom: Fifty Years after Vatican II's *Dignitatis Humanae*." This series was organized and convened in anticipation of the fiftieth anniversary of this landmark Catholic document that was promulgated at the closing of the final session of the Second Vatican Council on December 7, 1965.

As rector of St. Charles Seminary, I am very pleased to present this small yet noteworthy volume on the impact of this important document in the post–Vatican II era. The lectures themselves were delivered on March 17, March 24, April 14, and April 21, 2015. They were very well received and had an average attendance of about 150 people. The lectures were open to the general public and drew people of a variety of religious backgrounds from Philadelphia and its environs. Each lecture was followed by a period for questions and answers and an additional opportunity to meet with each of the presenters in a more personal manner over refreshments. Having attended the lectures myself and introduced each of them with a prayer for religious liberty provided by the United States Conference of Catholic Bishops, I can personally attest to the high quality of their content and the enthusiasm generated among the listening audience.

With the publication of these lectures, I wish to thank all the presenters for their willingness to participate in this series and for their outstanding contributions to the continuing search for religious freedom. I also wish to thank Fr. Dennis Billy, the present holder of the Krol Chair, for organizing the series and gathering the lectures into this present volume. Thanks also go to Deacon Stephan Isaac, research assistant; Michelle Lesniak, secretary; and Laura Verdi, coordinator of communications and marketing at the seminary, for the assistance they gave in making the series such a great success.

The threat to religious liberty in the world today and in our own country should not be underestimated. If care is not taken, the freedoms that allow us to practice our religious beliefs without governmental controls or outside interference could easily be eroded and eventually rendered lifeless. It is my hope that these lectures will serve as a catalyst for further study, reflection, and action in regard to what is, by all accounts, one of the most pressing issues of our present age.

+Most Reverend Timothy C. Senior
Rector, St. Charles Borromeo Seminary, Overbrook

Introduction

Dennis J. Billy, CSsR

Welcome to St. Charles Seminary and to our lecture series entitled "Continuing the Search for Religious Freedom: Fifty Years after Vatican II's *Dignitatis Humanae*." My name is Fr. Dennis Billy; I am the current holder of the Krol Chair, one of the seminary's two endowed chairs, and the main organizer of the series.

If I may, I will begin with a brief historical note about John Cardinal Krol, after whom the chair of moral theology at St. Charles Seminary is named and whose memory this lecture series honors. Cardinal Krol was the Archbishop of Philadelphia from 1961 to 1988 and President of the National Conference of Catholic Bishops from 1971 to 1974. He attended all four sessions of the Second Vatican Council, was a member of the council's central coordinating committee, and was one of its six permanent undersecretaries. Inasmuch as he was one of the main organizers of the council's agenda and the English-speaking secretary for the sessions, the various drafts of the document on religious freedom crossed his desk several times. It was through his administrative prowess that, after some very intense debate, the document eventually found its way to the floor for consideration, discussion, and ultimately a vote.

For this series, we have put together an impressive list of speakers to celebrate the fiftieth anniversary of the Declaration on Religious Freedom, which was promulgated on December 7, 1965, at the close of the council's fourth and final session; which Pope Paul VI identified as a major text, one of the council's greatest documents; and which was typically referred to as "The American Document," on account of the overwhelming support it had from the American bishops at the council and the influence of Jesuit Fr. John Courtney Murray, one of the document's major framers. According to Avery Cardinal Dulles, one of the foremost systematic theologians of the twentieth century, it is "the only document of Vatican II that explicitly claims to be a development of doctrine."[1]

Our first lecture, "Of Human Dignity: The Declaration on Religious Liberty at Fifty," by Archbishop Charles J. Chaput of Philadelphia, focuses on the present trials and future challenges involved in the search for religious freedom today. Archbishop Chaput is well suited to address this topic, since he is widely known as a leading voice for religious liberty in both the national and the international arena.

Our second lecture, "Continuing the Search for Religious Freedom: The American Perspective," by William P. Mumma, President of the Becket Fund for Religious

---

1   Avery Cardinal Dulles, SJ, "*Dignitatis Humanae* and the Development of Catholic Doctrine," in Kenneth Grasso and Robert P. Hunt, eds., *Catholicism and Religious Freedom: Contemporary Reflections on Vatican II's Declaration on Religious Liberty* (Lanham, MD: Rowman and Littlefield, 2006), 43.

Liberty, examines the difficulties facing American citizens in their efforts to preserve their religious liberties against the intrusions of their government. Mr. Mumma comes with a wide range of experience in dealing with the legal issues involved in our search for religious liberty.

Our third lecture, "Religious Liberty and the Human Good," by Robert P. George of Princeton University, uses Catholic natural-law reasoning to present religious liberty as a basic human good necessary for the well-being and fulfillment of the human person. One of the leading proponents of the new natural-law theory, Professor George presently serves as the Chairman of the United States Commission on International Religious Freedom.

Our fourth and final lecture, "Continuing the Search for Religious Liberty: The Contribution of *Dignitatis Humanae*," by Archbishop William E. Lori of Baltimore, shows how the Declaration on Religious Liberty sheds light on the Church's mission of evangelization and thereby assists the Church in promoting a just and peaceful society in the face of current threats to religious freedom. As Chair of the Ad Hoc Committee for Religious Liberty of the United States Conference of Catholic Bishops, Archbishop Lori has been at the forefront of the Church's struggle to keep the torch of religious liberty burning brightly in our country and beyond.

The purpose of this lecture series is to celebrate a document that has produced a deep and lasting effect on the Catholic imagination, one that has moved the Church to the front lines of a perennial struggle. This struggle has intensified dramatically in recent years and may prove to be the major challenge facing the Church in years to come. The lectures in this series delve deeply into the Church's stance on religious liberty and demonstrate the relevance of its teaching for the challenges of today's world. They present religious liberty as a basic human good, a right given not by man but by God, an intrinsic quality of the person that promotes human dignity and a just and peaceful social order.

NB: To preserve the power and immediacy of each speaker's oral presentation, this volume preserves the style and idiom as he spoke on the evening of his lecture. A video recording of each lecture was made, and these recordings may be accessed through the St. Charles Borromeo Seminary website (http://www.scs.edu).

LECTURE ONE

Of Human Dignity:
The Declaration on Religious Liberty at Fifty

+Most Reverend Charles J. Chaput, OFM Cap.

Vatican II ended in December 1965 with an outpouring of enthusiasm and hope. The council's hope was grounded in two things: a renewed Catholic Faith, and confidence in the skill and goodness of human reason.

Half a century has passed since then. A lot has happened. The world today is a very different place from the world of 1965. And much more complex. That's our reality, and it has implications for the way we live our faith, which is one of the reasons we're here tonight.

Hope is one of the great Christian virtues. Christians *always* have reason for hope. As we read in John 3:16, "God so loved the world that he gave his only son, that he who believes in him should not perish but have eternal life." God is alive. God loves us. God never forgets us.

But Christians also need to see the world as it really is, so as to better bring it to Jesus Christ.

In some ways, the council's Declaration on Religious Liberty—*Dignitatis Humanae* in Latin, or "Of Human Dignity" in English—is the Vatican II document that speaks most urgently to our own time. The reason is obvious. We see it right now in the suffering of Christians and other religious believers in many places around the world.

Pope Paul VI, who promulgated *Dignitatis Humanae*, saw it as one of the most important actions of the council. It changed the way the Church interacts with states. And it very much improved the Church's relations with other Christians and religious believers. So I'm grateful to Fr. Billy and Bishop Senior for organizing these talks on the declaration. And I'm glad to offer my own thoughts this evening.

My job tonight is to give an overview of religious liberty issues: the problems we currently have, and the ones we'll face in the years ahead. I'll do that in three parts. First, I'll outline what the Church teaches about religious freedom. Second, I'll list some of the key religious liberty challenges heading our way. Third, I'll talk about why the council was right. Not just right in its teaching about religious liberty, but right in its spirit of hope. And that spirit of hope needs to live in our hearts when we leave here tonight.

So let's turn first to what the Church teaches about religious freedom. And we should start by recalling the nature of the world that the Church was born into.

One of the themes of the Enlightenment in the eighteenth century, which still has great influence today, was a kind of "anything but Jesus" attack on religious superstition, along with a special distaste for the legacy of the Catholic Church. Enlightenment philosophers wanted to recover the habits of reason and learning they thought were embodied in ancient classical culture. But this is rich in irony, because the classical age itself was deeply religious at every level of life. The gods were everywhere in daily routines and civic power.

To put it another way: Early Christians weren't hated because they were religious. They were hated because *they weren't religious enough by Pagan standards.* They weren't killed because they believed in God. They were killed because they didn't believe in the *authentic* gods of the city and empire. In their impiety, they invited the anger of heaven. They also threatened the well-being of everyone else, including the state. The emperor Marcus Aurelius—one of history's great men in terms of intellect and character—hated the Christian cult. He persecuted Christians not for their faith, but for what he saw as their blasphemy. In refusing to honor the traditional gods, they seemed to threaten the security of the state.

Why does this matter? The reason is simple. T. S. Eliot liked to argue that "no culture has appeared or developed except together with a religion." Nor can a culture survive or develop for long without one.[1] Christopher Dawson, the great historian, said the same. Religious faith, whatever form it takes, gives a vision and meaning to a society. In that light, pagans saw the early Christians as a danger, because they were. Christianity shaped an entirely new understanding of sacred and secular authority. Christians prayed for the emperor and the empire. But they would not worship the empire's gods.

For Christians, the distinction between the sacred and the secular comes straight from Scripture. In the Gospel of Mark, Jesus himself sets the tone when he

---

1   T. S. Eliot, *Notes Towards the Definition of Culture* (New York: Harcourt, Brace and Company, 1949), 13, 28.

tells us to render unto Caesar the things that are Caesar's, and to God the things that are God's.[2] But if that's true, then how do we explain sixteen centuries of the Church getting tangled up in state affairs? The details are complicated, but the answer isn't. Christians are amphibian creatures. God made us for heaven, but we work out our salvation here on earth. As the Roman world gradually became Christian, the Church gained her freedom. Then she became the dominant faith. Then she filled the vacuum of order and learning left by the empire's collapse. Religious and secular authority often mixed, and power is just as easily abused by clergy as it is by laypeople. The Church relied on the state to advance her interests. The state nominated or approved senior clergy and used the Church to legitimize its power.

Of course, the idea of the "state" is a modern invention. I use it here to mean every prince or warlord the Church has faced through the centuries. The point is this: over time, and especially after the Wars of Religion and the French Revolution, the "confessional state"—a state committed to advancing the true Catholic religion and suppressing religious error—became the standard Catholic model for government.

That's the history *Dignitatis Humanae* sought to correct by going back to the sources of Christian thought. The choice to believe *any* religious faith *must* be voluntary, even in a Catholic confessional state. Faith must be an act of free will, or it can't be valid. Parents make the choice for their children at baptism because they have parental authority. And it's important that they do so. But in the end, people who *don't* believe can't be forced

---

2   See Mk 12:13–17, 1 Pt 2:13–17, etc.

to believe, especially by the state. Forced belief violates the person, the truth, and the wider community of faith, because it's a lie.

Or to put it another way: error has no rights, but persons *do* have rights—even when they choose falsehood over truth. Those rights aren't given by the state. Nor can anyone, including the state, take them away. They're *inherent* in every human being by virtue of his or her creation by God. Religious liberty is a "natural" right because it's hardwired into our human nature. And freedom of religious belief, the freedom of conscience, is—along with the right to life—the most important right any human being has.

Having said this, we should recall what *Dignitatis Humanae* doesn't do. It *doesn't* say that all religions are equal. It *doesn't* say that truth is a matter of personal opinion or that conscience makes its own truth. It *doesn't* absolve Catholics from their duty to support the Church and to form their consciences in her teaching. It *doesn't* create license for organized dissent within the Church herself. It *doesn't* remove from the Church her right to teach, correct, and admonish the baptized faithful—including the use of ecclesial penalties when they're needed.

It also *doesn't* endorse a religiously indifferent state. It *doesn't* preclude the state from giving material support to the Church, so long as "support" doesn't turn into control or the negative treatment of religious minorities. In fact, the declaration says that government "should take account of the religious life of its citizenry *and show it favor* [emphasis added], since the function of government is to make provision for the common welfare" (no. 3).

Dignitatis Humanae states, "Religious freedom…has to do with immunity *from coercion in civil society* [emphasis added]. Therefore it leaves untouched traditional Catholic doctrine on the moral duty of men and societies toward the true religion and toward the one Church of Christ" (no. 1).

In the same passage, the Council Fathers stress that the "one true religion subsists in the Catholic and Apostolic Church," and that "all men are bound to seek the truth, especially in what concerns God and his Church, and to embrace the truth they come to know, and to hold fast to it" (no. 1).

To put it another way, *Dignitatis Humanae* is not just about freedom *from* coercion. It's also about freedom *for* the truth. The issue of truth is too easily overlooked.

The declaration took four drafts to complete. And it created a great deal of internal debate. Karol Wojtyla took part in Vatican II as a young bishop. He supported *Dignitatis Humanae* and became a great defender of religious freedom as John Paul II. But he *resisted* an early draft of the declaration *precisely* because it failed to make a strong connection between freedom and truth. The two go together.

What John Paul saw, and what the Council Fathers addressed in the declaration's final draft, is that words like goodness, freedom, and beauty don't mean anything without an anchor. They're free-floating labels—and very easily abused—unless they're rooted in a permanent order of objective moral truth.[3] We see that abuse of language every day now in our public discourse. But I'll come back to that in a moment.

---

3   For a fuller discussion, see Avery Cardinal Dulles, SJ, "John Paul II and the Truth about Freedom," *First Things*, August 1995.

In the mind of the council, religious liberty means much more than the freedom to believe whatever you like at home and to pray however you like in your church. It means the right to preach, teach, and worship in public and in private. It means a parent's right to protect his or her children from harmful teaching. It means the right to engage the public square through moral debate and works of social ministry. It means the freedom to do all of this without negative interference from the government, direct or indirect, though within the limits of "just public order."

Before we turn to the second part of my remarks, it's also worth noting that the full title of *Dignitatis Humanae* includes "On the Right of the Person and of Communities to Social and Civil Freedom in Matters Religious." Religious liberty belongs not just to individuals, *but also to communities.* Civil society precedes the state. It consists of much more than individuals. Alone, individuals are weak. Communities give each one of us friendship, meaning, a narrative, a history and a future. They root us in a story larger than ourselves or any political authority. This means that communities, and especially religious communities, are *strong*—and a necessary mediator between the individual and the state.

So let's move now to some issues we'll face in the years ahead. We'll start on the global level.

This year marks the one-hundredth anniversary of the Armenian Genocide. Armenians were the first nation in the world to adopt Christianity, in AD 301. Starting in 1915, Turkish officials deliberately murdered more than one million members of Turkey's Armenian

minority. The ethnic and religious cleansing campaign
went on into the 1920s. The victims were men, women,
and children. And they were overwhelmingly Christian.
Turkey has never acknowledged the genocide. It's one of
the worst unrepented crimes in history.

That kind of ugliness may sound impossible in our
day. But today we have our own tragedies—from church
bombings in Pakistan to the beheading of Christians in
North Africa. More than 70 percent of the world now
lives with some form of religious coercion. Tens of thou-
sands of Christians are killed every year for reasons linked
to their faith. North Korea has expunged religion from
its culture. China runs a sophisticated "security" network
to interfere with, and control, its religious communities.
Islamic countries have a very mixed record. Muslim
states range from relative tolerance to repression and
forced conversion of religious minorities. And the persecution has grown worse as Islam has radicalized. Shari'a
law claims to protect religious minorities. In practice, it
slowly smothers them.

Even in Europe, laws that interfere with religious
dress, practice, and public expression are on the rise. The
postwar founders of European unity—committed Catholic men like Alcide de Gasperi, Robert Schuman, and
Konrad Adenauer—*assumed* the Christian heritage of
their continent. Today the European Union ignores it,
and in practice, repudiates it. In doing so, Europe robs
itself of any real moral alternative to the radical Islam
spreading in its own countries.

And what about the United States? Compared to
almost anywhere else in the world, our religious freedom
situation is good. Religious believers played a very big
role in founding and building the country. Until recently,
our laws have reflected that. In many ways they still do. A
large majority of Americans still believe in God and still

identify as Christian. Religious practice remains high. But that's changing. And the pace will quicken. More young people are disaffiliated from religion now than at any time in our country's past. More stay away as they age. And many have no sense of the role that religious freedom has played in our nation's life and culture.

The current White House may be the *least friendly* to religious concerns in our history. But we'll see more of the same in the future—pressure in favor of things like "gay rights," contraception, and abortion services, and against public religious witness. We'll see it in the courts and in so-called "antidiscrimination" laws. We'll see it in "antibullying" policies that turn public schools into indoctrination centers on matters of human sexuality—centers that teach that there's no permanent truth involved in words like "male" and "female." And we'll see it in restrictions on public funding, revocation of tax exemptions, and expanding government regulations. We too easily forget that every good service the government provides comes with a growth in its regulatory power. And that power can be used in ways nobody imagined in the past.

We also forget Tocqueville's warning that democracy can become tyrannical *precisely* because it's so sensitive to public opinion. If anyone needs proof, consider what a phrase like "marriage equality" has done to our public discourse in less than a decade. It's dishonest. But it works.

That leads to the key point I want to make here. The biggest problem we face as a culture isn't gay "marriage" or global warming. It's not abortion funding or the federal debt. These are vital issues, clearly. But the deeper problem, the one that's crippling us, is that we use words like "justice," "rights," "freedom," and "dignity" without any commonly accepted view of what these words mean.

We speak the same language, but the words don't mean the same thing. Our public discourse never gets down to what's true and what isn't, because it *can't*. Our most important debates boil down to who can deploy the best words in the best way to get *power*. Words like "justice" have emotional throw-weight, so people use them as weapons. And it can't be otherwise, because the religious vision and convictions that once animated American life are no longer welcome at the table. After all, what can "human rights" mean if science sees nothing transcendent in the human species? Or if science imagines a transhumanist future? Or if science doubts that a uniquely human "nature" even exists? If there's no *inherent* human nature, there can be no *inherent* natural rights—and then the foundation of our whole political system is a collection of empty syllables.

Liberal democracy doesn't have the resources to sustain its own purpose. Democracy depends for its meaning on the existence of some higher authority outside itself.[4] The Western idea of natural rights comes *not* just from the philosophers of the Enlightenment but, even earlier, from the medieval Church. Our Western legal tradition has its origins *not* in the Enlightenment but in the eleventh-to-twelfth-century papal revolution in canon law.[5] The Enlightenment itself could never have

---

4   Pierre Manent, *Tocqueville and the Nature of Democracy* (Lanham, MD: Rowman and Littlefield, 1996), 85–86. See also Robert Kraynak, *Christian Faith and Modern Democracy: God and Politics in the Fallen World* (Notre Dame, IN: University of Notre Dame Press, 2001) as well as Kraynak's essay "Justice without Foundations," *New Atlantis*, Summer 2001.

5   On the origin of natural rights, see Brian Tierney, *The Idea of Natural Rights: Studies on Natural Rights, Natural Law and Church Law, 1150–1625* (Grand Rapids, MI: Eerdmans, 1997).

happened outside the Christian world from which it emerged. In the words of Oxford scholar Larry Siedentop, "Christianity changed the ground of human identity" by developing and uniquely stressing the idea—in contrast to ancient pagan society—of the *individual* person with an eternal destiny. In doing that, "Christian moral beliefs emerge[d] as the ultimate source of the social revolution that has made the West what it is."[6]

Modern pluralist democracy has plenty of room for every religious faith and no religious faith. But we're lying to ourselves if we think we can keep our freedoms without revering the biblical vision—the uniquely *Jewish and Christian* vision—of who and what man is. Human dignity has only one source. And only one guarantee. *We're made in the image and likeness of God.* And if there is no God, then human dignity is just elegant words.

Earlier I said we need to leave here tonight with a spirit of hope. So let's turn to that now in these last few minutes before we have questions and discussion.

We need to remember two simple facts. In practice, *no* law and *no* constitution can protect religious freedom unless people actually believe in and live their faith—not just at home or in church, *but in their public lives.* But it's also true that no one can finally take our freedom unless we give it away. Jesus said, "I am the way, the truth, and the life" (Jn 14:6). He also said, "You will know the truth,

On the roots of the Western legal tradition, see Harold Berman, *Law and Revolution: The Formation of the Western Legal Tradition* (Cambridge, MA: Harvard University Press, 1985).

6   Larry Siedentop, *Inventing the Individual: The Origins of Western Liberalism* (Cambridge, MA: Harvard University Press, 2014), 352–353.

and the truth will make you free" (Jn 8:32). The Gospel of Jesus Christ is for *people who want to be free*, "free" in the truest sense. And its message is meant for all of us, for all men and women—unless we choose to be afraid.

Looking back over the past fifty years, and even at our lives today, I think it's too easy to see the problems in the world. It's too easy to become a cynic.

There's too much beauty in the world to lose hope; too many people searching for something more than themselves; too many people who comfort the suffering; too many people who serve the poor; too many people who seek and teach the truth; too much history that witnesses, again and again, to the mercy of God, incarnate in the course of human affairs. In the end, there's too much evidence that God loves us, with a passion that is totally unreasonable and completely redemptive, to *ever* stop trusting in God's purpose for the world, and for our lives.

The Second Vatican Council began and ended in the aftermath of the Holocaust and the worst war in human history. If there's an argument to be made against the worthiness of humanity, we've made that argument ourselves, again and again down through the centuries, but especially in the modern age. Yet every one of the council documents is alive with confidence in God and in the dignity of man. And there's a reason. God makes greatness, not failures. He makes free men and women, not cowards. The early Church Father Irenaeus said that "the glory of God is man fully alive." I believe that's true. And I'd add that the glory of men and women is their ability, with God's grace, to love as God loves.

And when that miracle happens, even in just one of us, the world begins to change.

LECTURE TWO

Continuing the Search for Religious Freedom: The American Perspective

William P. Mumma

Let me begin by thanking all of you. It is an honor to be here. Last week His Excellency Archbishop Chaput opened this series. In three weeks, the legendary Professor Robert George will take this stage, and four weeks from now His Excellency Archbishop Lori will speak.

You see, it has been just four years since the Board of the Becket Fund for Religious Liberty asked me to quit my job on Wall Street in order to run this public interest law firm that defends religious liberty for people of all faiths. I was surprised at the request, as I am not a lawyer, and frankly I had no particular knowledge of constitutional law.

In my role at the Becket Fund, I travel frequently around the United States, meeting people from many religious communities. There is no question that anxiety about religious freedom in America is growing, fed by stories of school children punished for bringing their Bible to class, CEOs or fire chiefs losing their jobs because they publicly support traditional marriage, Catholic nuns facing government fines for refusing to supply abortion coverage to employees, and of course the annual fights over Christmas trees in the public square. And I can attest that these are not rare events blown out of proportion by the media. Ill treatment of religious belief and expression—at all levels of government—is far too common.

And yet, in my travels and discussions I find that often—too often—people seem to have made the journey from absolute complacency about religious freedom to total despair in a single bound. I attribute this melancholy to an overreliance on "golden age" stories. They run something like this:

> Americans came to this country seeking religious freedom—to worship as they please and allow others to do the same. Our Founding Fathers understood this, and made religious freedom the first freedom. For two hundred years that freedom was honored until secularists broke the compact and discarded the long-standing legal and societal protection of religious liberty for all.

There is some truth to this story, but prettified versions of our past history can make our current challenges seem surprising and unbearable. Catholics in particular should know there is more to the story. Religious freedom was not a gift we got at the country's baby shower—wrapped and sporting a pretty bow. It is something that has been constructed over the life of the republic and has required regular repair and periodic renovation.

To begin, let me offer three quick observations and then lay out a very brief history of the religious liberty struggle in America. After that I will take a look at what is happening right now and where I think the fight may be heading. First the observations:

1. Americans have embraced the term "separation of church and state" for over two hundred years. But its meaning has always been contested. Archbishop Chaput spoke of the dishonest use of language that is so destructive in our times. But even before this degradation of language, there was confusion about this particular term. We all love religious liberty; we just don't agree on what it is.

2. The current struggle over religious liberty is not unique—in some aspects, it looks much like quarrels common 150 years ago. However, it has shed some of the defining elements of past struggles (most notably the animosity between Protestants and Catholics) while acquiring new, powerful drivers of the conflict.

3. It is a mistake to lay the blame for the fight over religious liberty on the doorstep of the Supreme Court. The court plays an important role, but it does not operate in a vacuum. The court is ultimately driven by the opinion of the country—especially the opinion of the cultural elites—concerning religion and its relationship to the government.

Let me pause for a moment here because some of you might have balked at my use of the term "elites." This is another word that is commonly used but lacks a common meaning. For the purpose of this talk, the cultural elites are those who have power and status *and* are actively engaged in shaping the views and opinions of society—less about money and more about influence.

With these observations in mind, let me start by noting that at the Constitutional Convention religious liberty was not a hot topic—it was not the subject of fierce debate or the generator of any famous compromises. This was largely because it was not seen as an issue for the national government. When the First Amendment addressed religious liberty, it was essentially as a jurisdictional issue, constraining Congress but not the states. Beyond this jurisdictional consideration, the issue of religious liberty was not particularly pressing.

It was in the context of the bitterly contested 1800 election campaign and its aftermath that the first salvo of the political fight over religious liberty in the new republic was fired. Accused of deism/atheism by Congregationalist ministers supportive of the opposing party, Thomas Jefferson wrote his famous "Letter to the Danbury Baptists," in which he linked the language of the First Amendment to his famous metaphor:

> I contemplate with sovereign reverence that act of the whole American people which declared that their legislature should [now quoting the First Amendment] "make no law respecting an establishment of religion, or prohibiting the free exercise thereof," [and Jefferson continues in his own words] thus building a wall of separation between Church and State.[1]

Fifty years later, this letter was employed as evidence of the shared consensus of the drafters of the Constitution, and the metaphor of a wall of separation figured

---

1   Daniel L. Dreisbach, *Thomas Jefferson and the Wall of Separation between Church and State* (New York: New York University Press, 2002), 148.

prominently in Supreme Court decisions in the twentieth century. But at the time it was part of a political
battle—not a statement of shared belief—and Jefferson
hoped to employ it to weaken his opponents. He was
essentially hoping to silence clergy that were preach-
ing against his administration. As it was, the separation
metaphor did not take flight, largely because theological
disputes about separation (City of God vs. City of Man
considerations) made religious leaders uneasy.

What shifted the religious liberty issue into a central dispute was the growth in Catholic immigration.
When Jefferson wrote his letter in 1802, the Catholic
population of the United States was just over 1 percent.
By 1850 it was 7 percent, and it increased to 16 percent
by the end of the century. Ground zero of the collision
between Catholics and Protestants in the 1850s was the
public schools. Parents naturally wanted their children
to be educated in their faith. Protestants were the overwhelming majority, and as a rule they compromised on
denominational disputes when it came to instruction in
the public schools. They read from the King James Bible,
without commentary, and provided instruction in a nondenominational (Protestant) Christianity.

As you can imagine, Catholics resented this solution,
and the bishops responded by opening Catholic schools.
The rest of the century was marked by constant quarrels
about public funding for Catholic schools and compul-
sory attendance at public schools.[2]

---

2   For an excellent review of the conflict between Catholics and
    Protestants over public education, see Michael McConnell, John
    Garvey, and Thomas Berg, *Religion and the Constitution*, third
    edition (New York: Wolters Kluwer Law and Business, 2011),
    382–395.

These fierce debates over religion in schools spilled into municipal and state elections (and eventually national politics). In response, the Protestant majority advanced the idea that democracy required citizens capable of making free decisions—free, that is, from ecclesiastical oversight or interference. By this standard, Catholics were considered unfree—bound to obey Rome and priests. Therefore, a rising Catholic population was not just a religious threat but also a threat to democracy.

From this political dispute emerged a consensus shared by the (mostly Protestant) elites and a majority of the population. Under this thinking, separation of church and state meant the separation of ecclesiastical authority from government. A commingling of government and religion (as in the public schools) did not violate the separation of church and state as long as religion was not "sectarian"—meaning citizens relied not on the authority of their clergy but instead on the authority of individual conscience, formed through reading the Bible. This formula excluded Catholics while leaving the door open for most other Christians.

The constitutionality of this understanding of church/state separation was not challenged in court. It couldn't be. The First Amendment applied only to the federal government, and the federal government did not run schools.

This consensus—let's call it separation of church and state, but not separation of religion and state—was held by the Protestant majority. Yet it was certain to face continued challenges as the Catholic population continued to grow. But even before further immigration upset the balance, new religious movements challenged this consensus.

As the nineteenth century progressed, the nation's elites grew increasingly enamored of various "freethinker" movements (e.g., scientific theism). These secular liberals (as they called themselves) were not satisfied with a formulation of church and state that merely excluded Catholics—though they certainly did not like Catholicism. They were seeking a more complete separation of Christianity and the state. Aware of the fact that the First Amendment did not apply to the states—and did not include the actual phrase—they sought an amendment to the Constitution that would explicitly require separation at all levels of government.

The public, including Catholics, was not interested in adopting this new definition for separation of church and state—authored by atheists and intended to eliminate religion from the public square—and by the end of the 1880s, the amendment movement had failed. Secularists abandoned the public campaign and set out to persuade the courts and the culture to embrace their view of church/state separation.

Meanwhile, the power of church/state separation was enlisted in the nativist cause. The Ku Klux Klan employed the phrase as a key component of their platform. By the time forty thousand hooded Klansmen marched down Pennsylvania Avenue in 1925, separation of church and state was synonymous with American patriotism.

So, the idea of church/state separation by this point was unchallengeable, but the definition was still wide open for debate. Religious pluralism continued to be the likeliest force for changing the definition. Following WWII, Catholics finally reached 25 percent of the population. In addition, the Nazi regime discredited anti-Semitism and put a different light on the exclusion of Jews from the consensus. But it was the secularists who would ultimately force the shift. Having failed in 1880 to amend the Constitution, they found greater success in amending the culture. Secularists were increasingly present among the ranks of America's elites.

The flash point was once again public schools. After one hundred years of debates over public funding for religious schools, in 1947 the Supreme Court entered the arena. *Everson v. Board of Education* was about bus money for Catholic schools, and it seemed like a rerun of arguments from the 1840s. But the court did three things of note: For the first time, it applied the religious freedom clauses of the First Amendment to states and their subdivisions; it offered a form of neutrality toward religion as the basis for applying the establishment clause; and it raised separation of church and state to the status of a constitutional principle.

The opinion was written by Justice Hugo Black (who was a one-time member and continued supporter of the KKK).[3] But if the court expected that this opinion would allow the old consensus supporting separation to survive into the new era, it was putting new wine into old wineskins. Essential to the old nineteenth-century consensus was the idea that separation of church and state did not exclude the teaching of a nondenominational Protestant Christianity in public schools. But the Supreme Court decision to establish a doctrine of neutrality toward all religion while elevating the "wall of separation" to a constitutional principle put it on a collision course with the old consensus. And, by extending the First Amendment

---

3   Justice Black's history with the KKK is described in detail in Philip Hamburger, *Separation of Church and State* (Cambridge, MA: Harvard University Press, 2002), 422–434.

to the states, it was ensuring that the collision, when it came, would be of nationwide significance.

Within fifteen years, the wineskin burst with the 1962 decision on school prayer. The decision came as a highly unpleasant shock to the public—but not to the cultural elites. Professor Steven Smith says it best: "From the perspective of those for whom the secularist view had already become virtually axiomatic, in elevating the new view to Constitutional status, the Court was doing nothing more than clearly articulating what must always have been true."[4]

The 1880 amendment drive is the key. Secularism was not something new to the elites. It had been sufficiently strong eighty years before the 1962 court decision to drive a national political movement. Since then it had become the dominant force in intellectual circles.

And this points to why I say the Supreme Court is an important player but not the controlling factor in the debate. The court reflects the view of the cultural elite. For the first 150 years, that elite was not secularist and the court reflected their religiously flavored view of separation of church and state. It wasn't particularly favorable to Catholics or non-Christians, but it wasn't hostile to religion. As the elites shifted to embrace secularism, the court reflected that shift.

So what, if anything, is different about this new fight over church/state separation? The elite culture changed, and so the dominant consensus changed. There were quarreling and disputes between those who ascribed to the prevailing view and those who didn't. It seems familiar in the context of the history I just reviewed. Shouldn't

---

4   Steven D. Smith, *The Rise and Decline of American Religious Freedom* (Cambridge, MA: Harvard University Press, 2014), 122.

we view this as just another chapter in the same dispute? The teams have changed, but it's still World Series baseball?

So, is the latest version of church/state dispute just another season in a never-ending contest? I think there are two key differences.

First, the old consensus was unpalatable to specific religious minorities—Catholics, Jews, and non-Christians. The new consensus is unpalatable to the general religious majority (Christians of all denominations and non-Christians alike). A state that tramples on the religious convictions of a minority may be unfair, though it is not necessarily unstable. But a government that ignores the religious convictions of a majority of its population runs a much bigger risk. It is a highly unstable system.

We have seen this. As the elites have struggled to persuade or coerce the majority to accept their proposed new consensus for understanding the separation of religion and the state, the public has pushed back. Hence the launch of the culture wars, moral majority, etc.

The second significant difference in the contemporary religious liberty fight is this. The original consensus around church/state separation was essentially conservative. It was trying to preserve the old order in the face of immigrants with different religious beliefs. But the new vision of church/state separation is not similarly constrained. It is intent not on preserving but on transforming American society. Here let me quote from Professor Robert George: a large majority of elites hold to an orthodox secularism "that stand[s] for strict and absolute separation of not only church and state, but also faith and public life," going so far as to believe that "no legislation based on religiously informed moral convictions of legislators or voters" is legitimate.[5]

The new orthodoxy of church/state separation is fundamentally immodest in its scope. It is committed to completely segregating religion from government. In a world where "health, education, and welfare" are within the purview of the federal government, a strict separation (or segregation) of religion—right down to prohibiting all legislation based on religiously informed moral convictions—is tantamount to government banishment of religion.

As dramatic as this new formula seems, the elites who hold this view do not see themselves as imposing a new ideology on those who believe differently. Professor Steven Smith again: "Even as they aggressively assert themselves, modern liberal secular orthodoxies typically hold themselves out not as orthodoxies, but rather as being opposed to orthodoxy. As being 'neutral.'"[6]

Let me pause and summarize what I have said thus far.

- Americans love separation of church and state but don't agree on what it means.

- For 150 years Catholics and Protestants fought over it—mostly in regard to public schools.

- For the last fifty years, secularists have insisted that the fight is over and that the government now ensures neutrality at all levels.

- But neutrality turns out to be a decidedly non-neutral formula for strict separation that essentially

---

5 Robert P. George, *The Clash of Orthodoxies: Law, Religion, and Morality in Crisis* (Wilmington, DE: ISI Books, 2001), 6.

6 Smith, *Rise and Decline*, 137.

expels religion from any part of society touched by government, and since the government is growing, the space for religion is shrinking.

- The public has resisted this approach—but the cultural elites refuse to see this as the establishment of a new orthodoxy and are therefore unfazed by the resistance.

So where do we go from here? If we predict history by drawing straight lines, things look grim. Instead of moving toward an understanding of separation of church and state that might broaden to affirmatively embrace all religious belief, we are on a path that equates separation of church and state with the segregation or suppression of all religious activity. This may be neutral but it certainly isn't benign, and the public is sensing that something is not quite neutral about neutrality.

Three forces are routinely cited as pushing our country along this path in which neutrality and separation of church and state serve to undermine religion and religious liberty.

First is the apparent decline in religious belief, or at the very least, the growth of the "nones"—that is, those Americans who describe their religious affiliation as "none." Earlier I said that the current secular orthodoxy concerning the separation of church and state is unstable because it pits the elites against the majority of the public. But clearly, if the broad public joins the elites in their embrace of secularism, this new orthodoxy could be stable—and empowered to continue on a path to more radical segregation between faith and public life. This point is not lost on the cultural elites, and they have been active in using their commanding heights (public schools, universities, media, and entertainment) to promote this secular view.

A second factor that is pushing us toward this neutralist secular theocracy is the continued expansion of the government. We have seen a dramatic illustration of this with the Affordable Care Act. If the federal government dictates the parameters of health care for all Americans, any religious scruples that touch health care automatically become a church/state issue. Absolute separation of church and state leaves no room for compromise, and thus religious scruples must be banished from health care: abortion, contraception, euthanasia, embryonic stem cell therapies, cloning for organ transplants, transhumanism—it doesn't matter. If health care is in the domain of the state, religious morality cannot be present even as an underlying rationale for considering rules.

And it is not just health care. Everywhere the government extends its reach, this dynamic will be repeated. The Becket Fund currently is defending a Native American preacher whose bald eagle feather was seized in an undercover sting operation conducted at a powwow by the Fish and Wildlife Service[7]—I am not kidding! When the government enters the room, religion must exit through the back door.

The final force at work pushing us toward a dark future is the movement to establish the redefinition of sexual morality as a civil right rooted in the Constitution. At first glance, this might not seem sinister—even if it may not seem desirable (after all, it sounds like it will simply add to our rights). Unfortunately, this is not

---

[7] The Becket Fund for Religious Liberty, "McAllen Grace Brethren Church v. Jewell," March 12, 2015, http://www.becketfund.org/mcallen-grace/.

emerging as an added right but as an either/or proposition (with the government putting its thumb on the
scale). Secular orthodoxy rejects legislation based on
religiously informed moral convictions of voters as a
violation of separation of church and state. Traditional
sexual morality is undoubtedly rooted in religious beliefs
and traditions going back centuries. So by this logic, the
appearance of traditional sexual morality in any law or
government regulation is essentially unconstitutional.
Meanwhile, the new sexual morality, which is not rooted
in religious beliefs, is now a constitutional right! When
the two clash, the "wall of separation between church
and state" declares that the loser must be the ethic rooted
in religious morality. It is an either/or proposition.

Wow, pretty grim. The youth are abandoning God,
the welfare state is banning the Church from cradle to
grave in the name of separation, and the sexual revolution is replacing the First Amendment.

But I am an optimist—not just hopeful in the
Christian sense, but truly optimistic. And here is why.

I was raised by a family that held no religious belief
of any kind. Mummas are Mennonite going back a few
generations, but not for my grandparents or parents. So I
was not raised a Christian, or in any other faith, and most
certainly not Catholic. I would have answered those
surveys as "none." But just like I suspect is true for so
many of those respondents, the box I really would have
checked—if such a response had been included among
the options—is "searching for God." The 20 percent of
the population who are "nones" are as much the human
material for a new awakening as they are the shock
troops for a new secularism.

And that picture of religious instability matches
the political picture—the public is not happy with the

definition of religious freedom offered by the cultural elites. Americans continue to love separation of church and state—it remains as powerful as ever—but they do not like the current version of this church/state divide.

I know this is true because at the Becket Fund we have closely examined confidential survey data. Not push polls that ask questions designed to get sound bites for PR campaigns (both sides do this), but rather sophisticated surveys with focus groups that try to get to the bottom of how Americans feel.

It turns out that about 12 percent of the country thinks religion is a problem and believes that the job of religious liberty is to protect people from religion. In other words, the establishment clause is a license for the government to drive religion from public life—and save the American people from religious bigotry. Of course, our elites are heavily represented in this 12 percent.

On the other side, 41 percent of Americans are religious believers who also support religious liberty. They are committed to their faith, believe that religion is good for society, and believe that freedom of religion is essential to our democratic republic. (So that is 12 percent on one side, 41 percent on the other.)

Another 18 percent are religious believers who are indifferent to religious liberty issues. They may be busy or they may have no interest in politics. Mostly they are not inclined to involve themselves in disputes.

That leaves 29 percent of the country. This group is interesting. They are mixed religiously (some are believers, some agnostics, some atheists). They are inclined to believe religion is a private matter and are suspicious of its role in public life, but they are not hostile. Their passion is reserved for liberty—liberty of all types, including religious liberty.

So let's do the math. Whether you add the religious believers together (41 percent and 18 percent) to get 59 percent, or add the religious liberty lovers and the liberty enthusiasts together (41 percent and 29 percent) to get 70 percent, or just go for the whole enchilada and add everyone but the ideologues together and get 88 percent—the numbers look bad for the secularists. That's the first point of optimism.

The second reason for optimism is that recent years have shown the Supreme Court to be relatively friendly to religious liberty. Remember, it was nearly seventy years ago that Justice Hugo Black authored the decision that launched disestablishment. And, of course, it has been over forty years since *Roe v. Wade*. But an argument can be made that the current court is open to reconsidering the religious liberty balance. In the last three years, Becket Fund attorneys have brought three religious liberty cases before the Supreme Court, and they won them all.

In 2012, the court ruled 9-0 in our *Hosanna-Tabor v. Equal Employment Opportunity Commission* case that religious organizations can choose their ministers without government interference. This was widely hailed as the most significant religious liberty decision in the past fifty years.[8]

Last year, in another landmark decision, *Burwell v. Hobby Lobby*, the court confirmed the right of private business owners to insist that government regulations accommodate their sincere religious beliefs.[9]

---

8   "Hosannas for the Court: A Unanimous Ruling for Religious Freedom, and a Rebuke to Obama," *Wall Street Journal*, January 13, 2012.

9   The Becket Fund for Religious Liberty, "Supreme Court Victory for Hobby Lobby," March 12, 2015, http://www.becketfund.org/hobbylobbyscotusvictory/.

Also just this year, with *Holt v. Hobbs*, the Supreme Court granted the Becket Fund its third landmark victory by unanimously ruling that prisons cannot arbitrarily ban peaceful religious exercise.[10]

In addition to these three highly positive decisions, during 2014, the Becket Fund won relief from the Supreme Court for the Little Sisters of the Poor and then again for Wheaton College, allowing them to continue to carry out their religious missions free from crippling IRS fines until their cases—and others—finish the legal journey.

So our own experience tells us that people are ready to be evangelized; sophisticated survey data show that the people aren't convinced about the secular orthodoxy; and victories in the higher courts achieved by the Becket Fund and others indicate that justices are not convinced either. These are the raw ingredients for optimism. But ingredients require something more—a recipe.

Throughout my talk I have returned to the idea that our countrymen embrace the principle of separation of church and state but cannot define it. To transform this public support and higher court openness into a new, benign consensus, we must provide this definition.

And this is where *Dignitatis Humanae* comes in. The declaration provides the explanation—the recipe—needed. Here is what the document asks governments to do:

1. Provide an effective constitutional guarantee of religious freedom. (Our First Amendment does that, and statutory provisions like the 1993 Religious

---

10 Hanna Smith, "Prisoner Beards and Religious Freedoms: What a Recent Supreme Court Decision Means for You," *Deseret News*, February 2, 2015.

Freedom Restoration Act reinforce that constitutional guarantee.)

2. Show favor to the religious life of the citizenry. (This is the essence of the Hobby Lobby decision. The religious convictions of citizens like the Green family must be treated favorably by the government, not seen as a barrier to be torn down.)

3. Honor the religious freedom of both individuals and communities. (The unanimous Supreme Court decision in *Hosanna-Tabor* directly affirmed the rights of religious communities.)

4. Impose restrictions on religious freedom according to judicial norms and in conformity with the objective moral order. (Prisons are a classic example of a domain in which government must regulate religious activity. But as our 9-0 decision in *Holt v. Hobbs* confirmed, these restrictions are not without boundaries.)

So all four of these principles in *Dignitatis Humanae* not only are foundational to the American system but have been affirmed in recent history.

We have a public that wants to support religious liberty. Our higher courts are open to well-structured arguments. And *Dignitatis Humanae* gives us a well-reasoned, spiritually grounded framework for defining what separation of church and state means.

Are we done? Almost. Permit me to strain this metaphor: we need cooks.

Dignitatis Humanae speaks not only to governments but also to individuals. It makes demands of the state and demands of the people.

1. Do not use religious liberty as a pretext for refusing to submit to authority.

2. Spread the Gospel, but with prudence and with patience for those in error and the ignorant. (In other words, do not fear or despise the "nones.")

3. Exclude every manner of coercion when it comes to faith.

These first three points require no explanation in an audience like this, so let me move to the last point.

4. Make the freedom needed for the Church to care for the salvation of men a preeminent concern.

I can't think of a better point with which to close my talk. The Church is asking us to make religious liberty a preeminent concern. We need to take action—persuading and educating our fellow citizens, advocating political protection of religion and religious freedom, and taking our disputes before the courts.

My experience at the Becket Fund in this regard is what has made me optimistic. I have the privilege of working with an inspired and idealistic team. Beyond that, I have traveled the country and met Americans— Catholics and non-Catholics—willing to make religious freedom a preeminent concern. I welcome all of you to join the Becket Fund in this essential work.

LECTURE THREE

Religious Liberty and the Human Good

Robert P. George

The starting points of all ethical reflection are those fundamental and irreducible aspects of the well-being and fulfillment of human persons that some philosophers refer to as "basic human goods."[1] These goods—as more than merely instrumental ends or purposes—are the subjects of the very first principles of practical reason that control all rational thinking with a view to acting, whether the acts performed are, in the end, properly judged to be morally good or bad.[2] The first principles of practical reason direct our choosing toward what is rationally desirable because humanly fulfilling (and therefore intelligibly available to choice), and away from their privations.[3] It

---

1   See John Finnis, *Natural Law and Natural Rights*, second edition (Oxford: Oxford University Press, 2011), chapters 3–4.

2   Germain Grisez, "The First Principle of Practical Reason: A Commentary on the *Summa Theologiae*, 1-2, Question 94, Article 2," *Natural Law Forum*, vol. 10 (1965), 168–196.

3   Ibid.

is, in the end, the integral directiveness of these principles that provides the criterion (or, when specified, the
set of criteria—the moral norms) by which it is possible to rationally distinguish right from wrong—what
is morally good from what is morally bad—including
what is just and unjust.[4] Morally good choices are choices
that are in line with the various fundamental aspects of
human well-being and fulfillment integrally conceived;
morally bad choices are choices that are not.

To say the very abstract things I've just said is simply
to spell out philosophically the point made by Martin
Luther King in his "Letter from Birmingham Jail" about
just and unjust laws—laws that honor people's rights
and those that violate them. You will, perhaps, recall that
the great civil rights champion anticipated a challenge
to the moral goodness of the acts of civil disobedience
that landed him behind bars in Birmingham. He anticipated his critics asking, How can you, Dr. King, engage
in willful law breaking, when you yourself had stressed
the importance of obedience to law in demanding that
officials of the southern states conform to the Supreme
Court's desegregation ruling in the case of *Brown v.
Board of Education*? Let's listen to King's response to the
challenge:

> The answer lies in the fact that there are two types
> of laws: just and unjust. I would be the first to advo-
> cate obeying just laws. One has not only a legal but
> a moral responsibility to obey just laws. Conversely,
> one has a moral responsibility to disobey unjust laws.
> I would agree with St. Augustine that "an unjust law
> is no law at all."

---

4   John Finnis, *Natural Law and Natural Rights*, 450–452.

Now, what is the difference between the two? How does one determine whether a law is just or unjust?

A just law is a man-made code that squares with the moral law or the law of God. An unjust law is a code that is out of harmony with the moral law. To put it in the terms of St. Thomas Aquinas: An unjust law is a human law that is not rooted in eternal law and natural law.

Any law that uplifts human personality is just. Any law that degrades human personality is unjust. All segregation statutes are unjust because segregation distorts the soul and damages the personality. It gives the segregator a false sense of superiority and the segregated a false sense of inferiority.[5]

So: just laws elevate and ennoble the human personality, or what King in other contexts referred to as the human spirit; unjust laws debase and degrade it. Now his point about the morality or immorality of laws is a good reminder that what is true of that which is sometimes called "personal morality" is also true of "political morality." The choices and actions of political institutions at every level, like the choices and actions of individuals, can be right or wrong, morally good or morally bad. They can be in line with human well-being and fulfillment in all of its manifold dimensions, or they can fail, in any of a variety of ways, to respect the integral flourishing of human persons. In many cases of the failure of laws, policies, and institutions to fulfill the requirements of morality, we speak intelligibly and rightly of a violation

---

5   Martin Luther King Jr., *Letter from Birmingham Jail* (New York: Harper Collins, 1994). The letter was written and originally published in 1963.

of human rights. This is particularly true where the failure is properly characterized as an injustice—failing to honor people's equal worth and dignity, failing to give them, or even actively denying them, what is their due.

But, contrary to the teaching of the late John Rawls and the extraordinarily influential stream of contemporary liberal thought of which he was the leading exponent,[6] I wish to suggest that good is prior to right and, indeed, to rights. Here is what I mean: To be sure, human rights, including the right to religious liberty, are among the moral principles that demand respect from all of us, including governments and international institutions (which are morally bound not only to respect human rights but also to protect them). To respect people, to respect their dignity, is to, among other things, honor their rights, including, to be sure, the right that we are gathered today to lift up to our fellow citizens and defend— the right to religious freedom. Like all moral principles, however, human rights (including the right to religious liberty) are shaped, and given content, by the human goods they protect. Rights, like other moral principles, are intelligible as rational, action-guiding principles because they are entailments and, at some level, specifications of the integral directiveness or prescriptivity of principles of practical reason that directs our choosing toward what is humanly fulfilling and enriching (or, as Dr. King would say, uplifting) and away from what is contrary to our well-being as the kind of creatures we are—namely, human persons.

And so, for example, it is relevant to the identification and defense of the right to life—a right violated by

---

6   John Rawls, "On the Priority of Right and Ideas of the Good," *Philosophy and Public Affairs*, vol. 17, no. 4 (1988), 251–276.

abortion, the killing of handicapped newborns and other physically or mentally disabled persons, the euthanizing of persons suffering from Alzheimer's disease and other dementias common among the elderly, and all acts of whatever type that involve the direct killing of innocent human beings, including the killing of captured enemy soldiers and the targeting of civilians in terror attacks, even in justified wars—that human life is no mere instrumental good but rather an intrinsic aspect of the good of human persons—an integral dimension of our overall flourishing.[7] And it is relevant to the identification and defense of the right to religious liberty that religion is yet another irreducible aspect of human well-being and fulfillment—a basic human good.[8]

But what is religion?

In its fullest and most robust sense, religion is the human person's being in right relation to the divine—the more than merely human source or sources, if there be such, of meaning and value. Of course, even the greatest among us in the things of the spirit fall short of perfection in various ways. But in the ideal of perfect religion, the person would understand as comprehensively and deeply as possible the body of truths about spiritual things, and would fully order his or her life, and share in the life of a community of faith that is ordered, in line with those truths. In the perfect realization of the good of religion, one would achieve the relationship that the

---

7   Germain Grisez, John Finnis, and Joseph M. Boyle Jr., *Nuclear Deterrence, Morality and Realism* (Oxford: Clarendon Press, 1987), 304–309.

8   On religion as a basic human good, see John Finnis, *Natural Law and Natural Rights*, 89–90.

divine—say God himself, assuming for a moment the truth of monotheism—wishes us to have with him.

Of course, different traditions of faith have different views of what constitutes religion in its fullest and most robust sense. There are different doctrines, different scriptures, different structures of authority, and different ideas of what is true about spiritual things and what it means to be in proper relationship to the more than merely human sources of meaning and value that different traditions understand as divinity.[9]

For my part, I believe that reason has a very large role to play for each of us in deciding where spiritual truth most robustly is to be found. And by reason here, I mean not only our capacity for practical reasoning and moral judgment but also our capacities for understanding and evaluating claims of all sorts: logical, historical, scientific, and so forth. But one need not agree with me about this in order to affirm with me that there is a distinct basic human good of religion—a good that is uniquely architectonic in shaping one's pursuit of and participation in all the basic human goods—and that one begins to realize and participate in this good from the moment one begins the quest to understand the more than merely human sources of meaning and value and to live authentically by ordering one's life in line with one's best judgments of the truth in religious matters.

If I am right, then the existential raising of religious questions, the honest identification of answers, and the fulfilling of what one sincerely believes to be one's

---

9   For a thoroughly informed and sensitive treatment of similarities and differences in the world's historical religions, see Augustine Di Noia, *The Diversity of Religions: A Christian Perspective* (Washington, DC: Catholic University Press, 1992).

duties in the light of those answers are all parts of the human good of religion—a good whose pursuit is an indispensable feature of the comprehensive flourishing of a human being. If I am right, in other words, then man is, as Becket Fund founder Seamus Hasson says, intrinsically and by nature a religious being—*homo religiosus*, to borrow a concept, or at least a couple of Latin words, from Eliade—and thus the flourishing of man's spiritual life is integral to his all-around well-being and fulfillment.

But if that is true, then respect for a person's well-being, or more simply respect for the person, demands respect for his or her flourishing as a seeker of religious truth and as a man or woman who lives in line with his or her best judgments of what is true in spiritual matters. And that, in turn, requires respect for his or her liberty in the religious quest—the quest to understand religious truth and order one's life in line with it. Because faith of any type, including religious faith, cannot be authentic—it cannot be *faith*—unless it is free, respect for the person—that is to say, respect for his or her dignity as a free and rational creature—requires respect for his or her religious liberty. That is why it makes sense, from the point of view of reason, and not merely from the point of view of the revealed teaching of a particular faith—though many faiths proclaim the right to religious freedom on theological and not merely philosophical grounds—to understand religious freedom as a fundamental human right.

Interestingly and tragically, in times past, and even in some places today, regard for persons' spiritual well-being has been the premise, and motivating factor, for *denying* religious liberty or conceiving of it in a cramped and restricted way. Before the leadership of the

Catholic Church embraced the robust conception of religious freedom that honors the civil right to give public witness and expression to sincere religious views (even when erroneous), in the document *Dignitatis Humanae* of the Second Vatican Council, some Catholics rejected the idea of a right to religious freedom based on the idea that "only the truth has rights." The idea was that the state, under favoring conditions, should not only publicly identify itself with Catholicism as the true faith but also forbid religious advocacy or proselytizing that could lead people into religious error and apostasy.

The mistake here was not in the premise: religion is a great human good, and the truer the religion the better for the fulfillment of the believer. That is true. The mistake, rather, was in the supposition made by some that the good of religion was not being advanced or participated in outside the context of the One True Faith, and that it could be reliably protected and advanced by placing civil restrictions enforceable by agencies of the state on the advocacy of religious ideas. In rejecting this supposition, the Fathers of the Second Vatican Council did not embrace the idea that error has rights; they noticed, rather, that *people* have rights, and they have rights even when they are in error.[10] And among those rights, integral to authentic religion as a fundamental and irreducible aspect of the human good, is the right to express and even advocate, in line with one's sense of one's conscientious obligations, what one believes to be true about spiritual matters, even if one's beliefs are, in one way or another, less than fully sound, and, indeed, even if they are false (DH, nos. 2–3).

---

10 See Kevin J. Hasson, *The Right to Be Wrong: Ending the Culture War over Religion in America* (New York: Encounter Books, 2005).

When I have assigned the document *Dignitatis Humanae* in courses addressing questions of religious liberty, I have always stressed to my students the importance of reading another document of the Second Vatican Council, *Nostra Aetate*, together with it. Whether one is Catholic or not, I don't think it is possible to achieve a rich understanding of the Declaration on Religious Liberty, and the developed teaching of the Catholic Church on religious freedom, without considering what the Council Fathers proclaim in the Declaration on Non-Christian Religions. In *Nostra Aetate*, the Fathers pay tribute to all that is true and holy, implying and then explicitly saying that there is much that is good and worthy in non-Christian faiths, including Hinduism and Buddhism, and especially Judaism and Islam. In so doing, they give recognition to the ways in which religion, even where it does not include the defining content of what the Fathers, as Catholics, believe to be religion in its fullest and most robust sense—namely, the Incarnation of Jesus Christ—enriches, ennobles, and fulfills the human person in the spiritual dimension of his being. This is to be honored and respected, in the view of the Council Fathers, because the dignity of the human person requires it. Naturally, the nonrecognition of Christ as the Son of God must count for the Fathers as a falling short in the non-Christian faiths, even the Jewish faith, in which Christianity is itself rooted and which stood according to Catholic teaching in an unbroken and unbreakable covenant with God—just as the proclamation of Christ as the Son of God must count as an error in Christianity from a Jewish or Muslim point of view. But, the Fathers teach, this does not mean that Judaism and Islam are simply false and without merit (just as neither Judaism nor Islam teaches that Christianity is simply false and without merit); on the contrary, these traditions enrich the lives of their faithful in their spiritual dimensions, thus contributing vitally to their fulfillment.

Now, the Catholic Church does not have a monopoly on the natural-law reasoning by which I am today explicating and defending the human right to religious liberty.[11] But the Church does have a deep commitment to such reasoning and long experience with it. And in *Dignitatis Humanae*, the Fathers of the Second Vatican Council present a natural-law argument for religious freedom—indeed, they begin by presenting a natural-law argument before supplementing it with arguments appealing to the authority of God's Revelation in Sacred Scripture. So let me ask you to linger with me a bit longer over the key Catholic texts so that I can illustrate by the teachings of an actual faith how religious leaders and believers, and not just statesmen seeking to craft national or international policy in circumstances of religious pluralism, can incorporate into their understanding of the basic human right to religious liberty principles and arguments available to all men and women of sincerity and goodwill by virtue of what Professor Rawls once referred to as "our common human reason."[12]

Let me quote at some length from *Nostra Aetate* to give you an appreciation of the rational basis of the

---

11 On natural law and religious freedom in the Jewish tradition, see David Novak, *In Defense of Religious Liberty* (Wilmington, DE: ISI Books, 2009). (Rabbi Novak kindly dedicated this fine work to me. Inasmuch as this is the first time I've had occasion to cite it in a publication, I am happy to have the opportunity to publicly thank him for what I consider to be a high honor.)

12 John Rawls, *Political Liberalism*, expanded edition (New York: Columbia University Press, 1993), 137.

Catholic Church's affirmation of the good of religion as manifested in various different faiths. I do this in order to show how one faith, in this case Catholicism, can root its defense of a robust conception of freedom of religion not in a mere *modus vivendi*, or mutual nonaggression pact, with other faiths, or in what the late Judith Shklar labeled a "liberalism of fear," or, much less, in religious relativism or indifferentism, but rather in a rational affirmation of the value of religion as embodied and made available to people in and through many traditions of faith. So here is what *Nostra Aetate* says:

> Throughout history even to the present day, there is found among different peoples a certain awareness of a hidden power, which lies behind the course of nature and the events of human life. At times there is present even a recognition of a supreme being or still more of a Father. This awareness and recognition results in a way of life that is imbued with a deep religious sense. The religions which are found in more advanced civilizations endeavor by way of well-defined concepts and exact language to answer these questions. Thus in Hinduism men explore the divine mystery and express it both in the limitless riches of myth and the accurately defined insights of philosophy. They seek release from the trials of the present life by ascetical practices, profound meditation and recourse to God in confidence and love. Buddhism in its various forms testifies to the essential inadequacy of this changing world. It proposes a way of life by which men can, with confidence and trust, attain a state of perfect liberation and reach supreme illumination either through their own efforts or by the aid of divine help. So, too, other religions which are found throughout the world

attempt in their own ways to calm the hearts of men by outlining a program of life covering doctrine, moral precepts and sacred rites. *The Catholic Church rejects nothing of what is true and holy in these religions* [emphasis added]. She has a high regard for the manner of life and conduct, the precepts and doctrines which, although differing in many ways from her own teaching, nevertheless often reflect truths which enlighten all men. Yet she proclaims, and is in duty bound to proclaim without fail, Christ who is the way, the truth and the life (Jn 1:6). In him, in whom God reconciled all things to himself (2 Cor 5:18–19), men find the fullness of their religious life.

The Church, therefore, urges her sons to enter with prudence and charity into discussion and collaboration with members of other religions. Let Christians, while witnessing to their own faith and way of life, acknowledge, preserve and encourage the spiritual and moral truths found among non-Christians.

The Church has also a high regard for the Muslims. They worship God, who is one, living and subsistent, merciful and almighty, the Creator of heaven and earth, who has also spoken to men. They strive to submit themselves without reserve to the decrees of God, just as Abraham submitted himself to God's plan, to whose faith Muslims link their own. Although not acknowledging Jesus as God, they revere him as a prophet; his virgin Mother they also honor, and even at times devoutly invoke. Further, they await the Day of Judgment and the reward of God following the resurrection of the dead. For this reason they highly esteem an upright life and worship God, especially by way of prayer, almsgiving, and fasting.

Over the centuries many quarrels and dissensions have arisen between Christians and Muslims. The sacred Council now pleads with all to forget the past, and urges that a sincere effort be made to achieve mutual understanding; for the benefit of all men, let them together preserve and promote peace, liberty, social justice and moral values.

Sounding the depths of the mystery which is the Church, this sacred Council remembers the spiritual ties which link the people of the New Covenant to the stock of Abraham.

The Church of Christ acknowledges that in God's plan of salvation the beginning of her faith and election is to be found in the patriarchs and in Moses and the prophets. She professes that all Christ's faithful, who as men of faith are sons of Abraham (cf. Gal 3:7), are included in the same patriarch's call and that the salvation of the Church is mystically prefigured in the exodus of God's chosen people from the land of bondage. On this account the Church cannot forget that she received the revelation of the Old Testament by way of that people with whom God in his inexpressible mercy established the ancient covenant. Nor can she forget that she draws nourishment from that good olive tree onto which the wild olive branches of the Gentiles have been grafted (cf. Rom 11:17–24). The Church believes that Christ who is our peace has through his cross reconciled Jews and Gentiles and made them one in himself (cf. Eph 2:14–16).[13]

---

13 *Nostra Aetate*, nos. 2–4.

Of course, from the point of view of any believer, the further away one gets from the truth of faith in all its dimensions—what the Council Fathers refer to in the passages I just quoted as "the fullness of religious life"—the less fulfillment one finds. But that does not mean that even a primitive and superstition-laden faith, much less the faiths of those advanced civilizations to which the Fathers refer, is utterly devoid of value, or that there is no right to religious liberty for people who practice such a faith. Nor does it mean that atheists have no right to religious freedom. The fundaments of respect for the good of religion require that civil authority respect (and, in appropriate ways, even nurture) conditions or circumstances in which people can engage in a sincere religious quest and live lives of authenticity reflecting their best judgments as to the truth of spiritual matters. To compel an atheist to perform acts that are premised on theistic beliefs that he cannot, in good conscience, share is to deny him the fundamental bit of the good of religion that is his, namely, living with honesty and integrity in line with his best judgments about ultimate reality. Coercing him to perform religious acts does him no good, since faith really must be free, and dishonors his dignity as a free and rational person. The violation of liberty is worse than futile.

Of course, there are limits to the freedom that must be respected for the sake of the good of religion and the dignity of the human person as a being whose integral fulfillment includes the spiritual quest and the ordering of one's life in line with one's best judgment as to what spiritual truth requires. Gross evil—even grave injustice—can be committed by sincere people for the sake of religion. Unspeakable wrongs can be done by people seeking sincerely to get right with God or the gods or their conception of ultimate reality, whatever it is. The presumption in favor of respecting liberty must, for the sake of human good and the dignity of human persons as free and rational creatures—creatures who, according to Judaism and Christianity, are made in the very image and likeness of God—be powerful and broad. But it is not unlimited. Even the great end of getting right with God cannot justify a morally bad means, even for the sincere believer. I don't doubt the sincerity of the Aztecs in practicing human sacrifice, or the sincerity of those in the history of various traditions of faith who used coercion and even torture in the cause of what they believed was religiously required. But these things are deeply wrong, and need not (and should not) be tolerated in the name of religious freedom. To suppose otherwise is to back oneself into the awkward position of supposing that violations of religious freedom (and other injustices of equal gravity) must be respected for the sake of religious freedom.

Still, to overcome the powerful and broad presumption in favor of religious liberty, to be justified in requiring the believer to do something contrary to his faith or forbidding the believer to do something his faith requires, political authority must meet a heavy burden. The legal test in the United States under the Religious Freedom Restoration Act is one way of capturing the presumption and burden: to justify a law that bears negatively on religious freedom, even a neutral law of general applicability, it must be supported by a compelling state interest and represent the least restrictive or intrusive means of protecting or serving that interest. We can debate, as a matter of American constitutional law or as a matter of policy, whether it is, or should be, up to courts or legislators to decide when exemptions to general, neutral laws should be granted for the sake of religious freedom, or to determine when the presumption in favor of religious freedom has been overcome. But the substantive matter of what religious freedom demands from those who exercise the levers of state power should be something on which reasonable people of goodwill across the religious and political spectrums can agree—precisely because it is a matter capable of being settled by our common human reason.

LECTURE FOUR

Continuing the Search for Religious Liberty: The Contribution of *Dignitatis Humanae*

+Most Reverend William E. Lori, STD

Introduction

Let me begin with warmest thanks for your very kind welcome. It is a privilege to be a part of this lecture series celebrating the fiftieth anniversary of *Dignitatis Humanae* (DH), the Declaration on Religious Liberty promulgated by the Second Vatican Council on December 7, 1965. My special thanks to you, Fr. Billy, and to the seminary community for your gracious invitation and your kind hospitality.

In approaching this podium I am following true experts in religious freedom, including Archbishop Chaput, who is both a colleague and a friend, as well as Professor George of Princeton and Mr. Bill Mumma of the Becket Fund. These speakers devote their considerable intellectual and spiritual capital and most of their waking hours to the defense of religious liberty. I am most grateful to them, as I am sure you are as well.

The way I see it, I'm the fourth one at bat and in baseball that would make me the cleanup batter—and usually the cleanup batter's job is to clear the bases. I'd say it'll take more than a Ryan Howard (the cleanup batter for the Phillies) to drive in the winning run against today's challenges to religious freedom.

So what is my single responsibility this evening? I think it is this: to invite you to reread DH, if you haven't done so already. And I will issue that invitation by citing what I think are its most enduring contributions to the ongoing search for religious freedom. That search, dear friends, continues to intensify. Abroad we see overt religious persecution, especially against Christians, in the Middle East, Africa, and elsewhere. Believers are dispossessed, exiled, enslaved, and beheaded by radical Islamist militants, especially those affiliated with ISIS. In the Western democracies, including the United States, religious liberty is under assault in the media, on college campuses, and through bad court decisions, laws, and regulations. Although DH is fifty years old, its teaching remains prophetic. It is as if the Council Fathers looked ahead to read the signs of our times. Now it is up to us to reread this Declaration on Religious Liberty for guidance in addressing threats to religious freedom, in helping to shape the Church's mission of evangelization, and in contributing to the formation of a society that is just and peaceful.

So this evening I will propose four of many contributions that DH has made to the ongoing quest for religious liberty, and along the way, I will mention how these contributions apply to our times. Here are the four points:

1. The very existence of the document itself is an enduring contribution to the Church's treasury of knowledge, teaching, and prophetic witness.

2. A second contribution is the link that DH makes between truth and freedom in explaining religious freedom as integral to human dignity.

3. A third is the way in which the document links reason and Revelation in explaining the origins of religious freedom and its roots in our Tradition.

4. And fourth is the enduring contribution of DH to the Church's mission of evangelization.

When I've finished, I'll be happy to take your questions.

The "Fact" of the Document

So let me begin with the first contribution of DH: the "fact" or the "existence" of the document itself (if I can put it this way). DH, of course, was not the first word the Church spoke about religious liberty. Pope Leo XIII championed the freedom of the Church in the context of his day, especially with the rise of various antireligious ideologies and political developments such as the Kulturkampf in Bismarck's Germany. Similarly, Pope Pius XI defended the religious freedom of the Church as totalitarian governments sprang up in Europe. So too Pope Pius XII defended the Church's liberty as well as the human rights and freedoms of the victims of World War II. Nonetheless, DH marks the first time the Church issued a magisterial document solely on the subject of religious freedom. It is the first time an ecumenical council dealt with religious freedom in such a sustained fashion and at such a high level of authority.

Why, then, did the council decide to deal with religious liberty? In convoking the council, John XXIII spoke not only of the progress of humanity but also of the immense crisis that was confronting society. When he said that the Church was in a period as tragic as any in her history, the saintly pontiff was surely referring to the bloody wars of the twentieth century, the totalitarian regimes, the threat of nuclear annihilation, and the rise of atheism. He proposed to bring the Church into closer contact with a conflicted global culture, first by looking deeply into her own Tradition and expanding it, and second by "reading the signs of the times and interpreting them in light of the Gospel" (*Gaudium et Spes*,[1] no. 4).

Among the human aspirations to which the council listened attentively was the yearning of the oppressed for freedom, including religious freedom. Further, the American bishops strongly believed that the experiment of religious freedom in the United States was exceptional and that it should be reflected in the deliberations of the council. As we shall later discuss, during the second session of the council, Francis Cardinal Spellman of New York brought with him Fr. John Courtney Murray, SJ, as his *peritus*, or expert, on religious liberty.

DH originated in the Secretariat for Promoting Christian Unity under the direction of Augustin Cardinal Bea, its first president. The document sought to do two things: first, to avoid the shoals of religious indifferentism, that is to say, the danger of describing religious freedom in such a way that the Church would seem to

---

1   Hereafter cited as GS.

be saying that one is free to choose one's religion because one religion is as good as another; second, to recognize the value of structuring society in such a way that the religious freedom of all citizens is protected. The council planners thought that the statements on religious liberty should be part of an eventual document on ecumenism and interfaith relationships, and in fact they devoted Chapter V of the first draft of that document to religious liberty. After all, the questions raised by religious liberty and by ecumenism were closely related. In treating ecumenism, the council Fathers would have to avoid indifferentism—i.e., relativizing the Catholic Church as merely one tradition among many—while promoting the crucial importance of Christian unity and interfaith understanding. In treating religious liberty, the council Fathers would again have to avoid indifferentism while defending the religious freedom of people everywhere. Speaking in favor of that very early draft on religious freedom, Bishop de Smedt of Belgium anticipated the debate on religious liberty that would take place on the council floor: "What, therefore, is meant in the text by 'religious freedom'? Positively, religious freedom is the right of the human person to the free exercise of religion according to the dictates of his conscience. Negatively, it is immunity from all external force in his personal relations with God."

By 1964, the council's central commission decided that the declaration on religious liberty should become a freestanding document. The draft was developed, amended, and debated in late September that same year, and a vigorous debate it was, with some forty-three council Fathers speaking. Some bishops serving in the Roman curia and most of the Spanish bishops opposed this still-early draft on the grounds that "the truth alone has a right to freedom whereas error may be 'tolerated' for the sake of avoiding a greater evil." Other council Fathers objected to assertions in the draft that the state is "incompetent" or even "benignly disinterested" in religious matters. Seeing such a view as a departure from the Church's constant teaching, they maintained that civil authority cannot be indifferent with regard to religion. Rather, it must take note of the moral law and Revelation as proposed by the Church, and then frame laws and policies accordingly. Still others, including some French bishops and Archbishop Karol Wojtyla of Kraków, criticized "the overly judicial" notion of religious freedom in that early draft, an assertion to which we will return later in this talk.

In the end, the conciliar debate about the document on religious freedom hinged on the question of "who man is"—and of his fundamental orientation toward God. It hinged on the innate "capacity" of the human being for truth in his search for God, a capacity that perdures in spite of man's sinfulness and his inability to save himself. Describing the work of Vatican II, Pope Benedict XVI said this: "In the great dispute about man which marks the modern epoch, the Council had to focus in particular on the theme of anthropology" (Pope Benedict XVI, address to Roman Curia, Dec. 2005). To be sure, the council brought forth the Church's teaching on Revelation, on Christ, on the Church in a very rich and beautiful way. And in doing so, the council allowed the Faith to shed its light on who the human person is and on the problems that humanity is facing. Thus, along with a doctrinal/theological line, one might also be able to trace an "anthropological line" in the conciliar documents, especially DH and *Gaudium et Spes* (see no. 22). In the debates about religious liberty and the Church in the modern world, a fuller, more "theological" account of the human person was advanced. Without discounting original sin, or personal sin, or indeed structural sin, the council, some would say, moved away from the view that man has a natural end and a supernatural end. According to that view, while man can know moral truth and even the existence of God by means of reason unaided by Revelation, nonetheless in his innate state man has only a nonrepugnance for the divine. In stating that Christ, the Word made flesh, in revealing the Father revealed man to himself and brought light most fully to man's dignity and destiny, the council signaled, it seems to me, a theologically richer view of man, one that includes his innate capacity for truth and his desire for God. The fault lines in the conciliar debate on religious liberty revolved around this question, and I will refer back to this point a few times later in my remarks.

It will be long debated whether DH represents a break with Tradition or whether it stands in continuity with Tradition. In issuing DH, however, the council Fathers were careful to say that it is not a break from Tradition but an organic development of it. DH is new insofar as it entertains the notion that the state is "incompetent" in religious matters, or to put it another way, that matters of religion are above the "pay grade" of civil officials and the government itself. DH is new insofar as it takes account of the diverse contemporary political arenas in which the Church "lives and moves and has her being," so to speak. Yet in maintaining that the Church of Christ "subsists" in the Catholic Church and in clarifying the relationship of truth and freedom in a way that corresponds to both the yearnings of the human spirit and the mission of the Church to proclaim the Gospel to the ends of the earth—the Church, reading the signs of the times, digs deep into her Tradition and develops it. In the end, DH offers the building blocks for a fully integrated and articulated vision of human dignity that seems more necessary than ever in an era of resurgent religious persecution and of liberal democracies that are compromising religious freedom. The words of Pope Francis to the European Parliament are instructive: "In the end, what kind of dignity is there without the possibility of freely expressing one's thought or professing one's religious faith?"

Truth and Freedom

This provides a segue into my second topic, namely, the contribution of DH to our understanding of the relationship between truth and freedom in the ongoing search for religious freedom. This will bring us to the heart of the conciliar debates that occurred as DH was being hammered out on the council floor and behind the scenes. The *dramatis personae* include Fr. John Courtney Murray, SJ, Archbishop Karol Wojtyla, and a number of French bishops, including Bishop Alfred-Jean-Felix Ancel, then Auxiliary Bishop of Lyon. What was the debate about?

Fr. John Courtney Murray, SJ.

The Second Vatican Council took place in the midst of what historians call "The American Century." It was a time of unparalleled American influence around the world. And by all appearances, the Church in the United States was also riding high. It had flourished in the context of the American religious freedom experiment, which included such features as limited government, constitutionally guaranteed freedoms, and the separation of church and state. In the American system, the state declared itself "incompetent" in religious matters, so long as there was not a compelling need for governmental intervention. Despite setbacks such as the 1947 Supreme Court decision *Everson v. Board of Education* (which misinterpreted the establishment clause), for the most part civil authorities seemed relatively well disposed to the Church, especially in regard to her leaders and institutions. Indeed, not only were Catholic parishes and institutions booming, Catholics themselves were advancing in mainstream society and the halls of power. No wonder the American bishops believed that the American Catholic experience had a lot to say to the rest of the Church.

In that context, Jesuit Fr. John Courtney Murray's thought was very influential. Ordained in 1920, he taught Trinitarian theology at Woodstock, the Jesuit theologate in Maryland, and was the longtime editor of *Theological Studies*, until his death in 1967. During World War II, in 1943, he helped draft an interfaith statement on postwar reconstruction known as the Declaration of World Peace. Among other things, this document argued for a constitutional arrangement between the German government and the Church, especially regarding taxation, and this arrangement continues to be operative. Over time, Murray became increasingly interested in church–state relations, and he authored a series of essays collected in his 1960 book *We Hold These Truths*.[2] There he argues for "a formally juridical concept" of religious freedom. What does he mean by this?

By this phrase he meant that the object of religious freedom is not to encourage and foster the values

---

2 John Courtney Murray, *We Hold These Truths: Catholic Reflections on the American Proposition* (New York: Sheed and Ward, 1960).

inherent in religious belief and practice. Such values, he says, are "judicially irrelevant." Rather, the object of religious freedom is simply to ensure that there are no undue constraints on individuals and religious groups in regard to the free pursuit of whatever is of value to them in their religion. Describing religious freedom as "the absence of constraint" or as "immunity" from it, Murray believed the "content" of religious freedom to be "negative." As conceived in the American Constitution, Murray tells us, religious freedom is not a rejection of but an abstraction from man's relationship with truth and with God. I don't think Murray used this image, but if you will, picture it this way: religious freedom means that the state is obliged to preserve and protect for each citizen what it sees as an "empty space" that individuals and groups can "fill up" by choosing to practice a religion or not. Murray advances this "negative" view of religious liberty for two primary reasons.

First, Murray says it fits well with the American idea of limited government. Religion is one of those spheres of human activity that the government acknowledges and protects from constraints. At the same time, the government refrains from entering into those spheres by imposing its own judgments, be they philosophical, moral, or theological. The government declares itself "incompetent" in such matters that are better left to individuals and those in free association with one another. And relying on the maintenance of a broad moral consensus among civil authorities, the culture at large, and the Church, Murray could read the First Amendment as "articles of peace." By that he meant that church and state are at peace because the state does not involve itself in matters spiritual, religious, and eternal. Of course, in real life, things are seldom so tidy!

Second, Murray argues that this "negative" concept of religious freedom, which by definition is free of theological presuppositions, is the best way to deal with the competing truth claims and religious claims in a pluralistic society. In those days, the United States was sometimes characterized not only as a Christian country but indeed as a Protestant Christian country, and at times religious liberty was framed by Protestant theological views. His effort to decouple religious liberty from such views, however, does not mean that Murray in any way subscribed to moral relativism or pragmatism. Father Murray himself was a natural-law theorist, and, as I mentioned, he saw the need for a moral consensus in society to support the articles of peace. As one author framed the question, the constitutional articles of peace need to be buttressed by societal "articles of faith," that is, a belief held by a critical mass of society, but not the state as such, that openness to religion is important to human flourishing.[3] It remains a matter of debate whether religious freedom, framed solely as immunity from coercion, is adequate to make an intrinsic link between freedom and moral responsibility. And while freedom from coercion is certainly fundamental to religious liberty, we may wonder if it is adequate when the societal moral consensus breaks down, as is arguably the case in many Western democracies, including our own. Does that result in a society filled with competing freedom claims with little hope of resolution, absent a moral consensus? Does that set the stage for the government's becoming the referee of those claims? . . . as seems to be happening in our country

---

3   Robert P. Hunt, "Two Concepts of Religious Liberty: *Dignitatis Humanae* v. the U.S. Supreme Court," in *Catholicism and Religious Freedom*, 37.

nowadays. And paradoxically, does this end up involving the government in religious matters, regarding which the government had declared itself "incompetent"?

Allow me to dwell on this point a bit more. Essential to human dignity is personal autonomy coupled with moral responsibility. Father Murray recognizes this very clearly in his writings. He writes that man, in his personal life, "is responsible for the conformity between the inner imperatives of his conscience and the transcendent order of truth."[4] He also says that man is responsible "for the conformity between his external actions and the inner imperatives of conscience." Yet, Fr. Murray goes on to assert that in the social order "where human rights are predicated, man's fulfillment of his personal responsibilities is juridically irrelevant." Murray is not saying that personal moral responsibility is irrelevant to society, but rather that it is juridically irrelevant as far as the state is concerned, because the state, as such, is "incompetent" to judge such matters. As the debate on DH unfolded, a pronounced difference of emphasis would emerge between those who believed that immunity from coercion was as far as the state could go in recognizing and guaranteeing religious freedom, and those who underscored that the state itself should guarantee religious freedom as grounded in a recognition of man's capacity for transcendent truth and the moral freedom to do that which a well-formed conscience dictates.

In spite of censures of the Holy Office in the 1950s regarding Murray's writings, at the urging of Francis Cardinal Spellman, Fr. Murray was invited to attend the

---

4   John Courtney Murray, "The Declaration on Religious Freedom," *Vatican II: An Interfaith Appraisal,* ed. John Miller, (Notre Dame, IN: University of Notre Dame Press, 1966), 571.

second and subsequent sessions of the council. Spellman and other American bishops used Murray as their *peritus* on religious liberty. Murray was not a council Father and thus did not intervene in the debate, but his ideas were put forth by a number of American bishops, and thus he made a substantial contribution to this important council document.

Archbishop Karol Wojtyla.

As the debate on DH proceeded, however, Murray's ideas on the "negative" conception of religious freedom were challenged. The challenger-in-chief was Archbishop Karol Wojtyla of Kraków. He took issue with the notion of religious freedom as mere "freedom from coercion" not because he thought it was wrong but because he thought it was incomplete. Of itself, it was indicative of a theologically inadequate view of the human person that was not appropriate for a Church document or even for the formation of a just society. He recognized that human rights, including religious freedom, are protected only when the state acknowledges the transcendence of man. A merely negative conception of religious freedom, emptied of all philosophical, religious, and moral content, does not fully take into account the transcendence of the human person, made by God in his likeness and endowed with reason and free will. But it is precisely in this transcendence that human rights have their origin. It is easy to see how a government could claim to be the grantor of religious liberty when religious freedom is thought of merely as protection from undue coercion. Yet, when religious freedom is linked to the inbuilt human search for truth and for God, we can more readily see that God, not the state, grants religious freedom. Ministering as he was in communist Poland, Archbishop

Wojtyla surely would have welcomed a newfound freedom from governmental constraints on the religious
rights of individual Poles and the rights of the Church's
institutions. Yet Wojtyla knew from his experience and
studies that religious freedom must rest on the basis of
transcendent human nature, which is open to a relationship with God and to truth perceived by a well-formed
conscience, which is the inner core, the inmost sanctuary,
of the human person (see GS, no. 16).

In one of his interventions, for example, Archbishop
Wojtyla asserted that immunity from coercion is more
concerned with religious toleration than with freedom.
Religious freedom does not mean merely that the state
allows religions to exist. Rather, it means that the state
acknowledges the right of the human person to the free
exercise of religion as something good for the human
spirit and for society itself. Wojtyla could see how the
merely negative notion of religious freedom could easily
slide into religious indifferentism and moral relativism.
In other interventions, he stated that this "negative" idea
of religious freedom alienates human dignity from its
foundation, namely, man's "natural" relationship with
God. Indeed, the right to religious freedom is primary
because it pertains to man's most fundamental relationship—his relationship with God. What's more, God
himself respects the freedom and capacity for truth that
he inscribed on our human nature. He manifests himself
to us in various ways but does not coerce us. Rather, he
seeks to elicit from us a free response of love. By rooting
religious liberty in human nature, in the heart of man,
DH intrinsically links religious freedom with the obligation to seek the truth. And so, the God-given ability to
choose is itself not indifferent to the truth but is oriented,
as St. Paul says, toward "whatever is honorable, whatever

is just, whatever is pure, whatever is lovely, whatever is gracious" (Phil 4:8). Thus it was that Archbishop Wojtyla spoke one of the most memorable sentences in all the deliberations of the Second Vatican Council: "*Non datur libertas sine veritate*"—there is no liberty without truth.

Wojtyla saw another danger in a "content-less" notion of religious liberty. Even when the neutrality of the state regarding religious claims is taken for granted, it can hardly be said that the state is neutral with regard to moral claims. For better or worse, all human laws and regulations have a moral dimension. Yet, when human freedoms are divorced both from man's subjective search for truth and from a societal acceptance of an objective moral law to which everyone is bound, everyone's rights are in danger of being violated. Without an underlying moral consensus, the opinions of the powerful will dominate not only the views but indeed the rights of the disadvantaged. Indeed, one of the criticisms of Murray's views is that the neutrality of the state toward religion in fact masks a relativism that makes society a place where competing claims bump up against one another with little hope of resolution. To be sure, it is imperative for us to enter into dialogue about such competing claims, but the success of such dialogue is diminished when there is a lack of shared values.

Wojtyla's concern that religious freedom be grounded in the objective moral order showed itself in yet another way during the conciliar debate on the text of DH. An early draft stated, somewhat baldly, that religious liberty could be limited by the requirements of public order. He called for that statement to be qualified in this way: the exigencies or requirements of public order cannot be limited merely by positive law, by purely man-made laws and regulations. Rather, such positive law and policies must be in accord with the natural law known by reason and known more clearly via Revelation. Indeed, religious freedom is violated when governmental authority constrains individuals or groups from following the natural law. In an era when religious freedom is beset by a host of governmental regulations clearly at odds with the Church's moral teaching and the natural law itself, the future pope's words not only ring true—they were prophetic.

Momentarily we shall see how Wojtyla also insisted that DH set forth not only what reason but indeed also Revelation teaches about the authentic meaning of religious freedom. His concerns about the philosophical, theological, and doctrinal adequacy of the text made it more responsive to the original intentions of the council itself, as described by Pope John XXIII. Reading the signs of the times in light of the Gospel, DH looks deeply into the Church's Tradition and indeed expands it. Archbishop Wojtyla helped to connect the newness of DH with Tradition while contributing here and in *Gaudium et Spes* to the development of the Church's teaching on the transcendent dignity of the human person— a dignity revealed most fully in Christ, the Word made flesh (GS, no. 22).

Illustrating the Two Streams of Thought in DH.

The influence of both Fr. Murray and Archbishop Wojtyla (and others) can be seen in the text of DH in its final form as one of the council's most important documents. Their influence is not mutually exclusive or conflicting but more properly should be viewed as complementary. Here are a few snippets to demonstrate this, beginning with a "Murray quote":

DH, no. 1: After declaring that the human person has a right to religious freedom, it says, "Such freedom consists in this, that all...should be immune from coercion on the part of individuals, social groups or any human power, so that no one is forced to act against his conscience in religious matters, or prevented from acting according to his conscience in private or in public, whether alone or with others, within due limits" (See also DH, no. 4). There immediately follow lines that reflect the influence of Wojtyla: "In addition, this Council declares that the right to religious freedom has its foundation in the very dignity of the human person as known from both the revealed word of God and reason itself" (DH, no. 2). The text goes on: "It is in accord with their dignity that all men and women, because they are persons, endowed with reason and free will and thus privileged with personal responsibility, are impelled by their nature and bound by a moral obligation to seek the truth, especially the truth concerning religion." And finally, "The right to religious freedom does not have its foundation in the subjective disposition of the person...but in his very nature" (DH, no. 2).

Let me also illustrate the influence of Murray and Wojtyla with two texts that pertain to the limitation of religious freedom in accordance with the demands of public order, beginning with a text that reflects the thought of Fr. Murray: "It is therefore an injustice to the human person, and to the very order of human existence established by God, for men to be denied the free exercise of religion in society when the just public order is preserved" (DH, no. 3). Later on, at no. 8, the text seems to reflect Wojtyla's concerns about grounding public-order limitations on religious freedom in the natural law: After stating that civil society has the right to protect itself from abuses that could be committed under the pretext of religious freedom, it adds, "This protection should not be provided in an arbitrary fashion...or by unjustly favoring one particular group, but according to juridical norms that conform to the objective moral order. Such norms are necessary for the effective protection of the rights of all citizens and the peaceful settlement of conflicts and rights."

The Debate Continues.

The debate about DH continues at many levels; it includes those who believe that the interventions of Wojtyla, Ancel, et al. gave definitive shape to the text and those who believe that those interventions were "add-ons" that enhanced but did not fundamentally change the teaching of DH that religious liberty is an essentially "negative" right, i.e., immunity from coercion. Unmistakably, both currents run through the text, though I would venture to say that the interventions of Wojtyla were decisive in providing DH with a theological anthropology that comports best with other conciliar texts, notably *Gaudium et Spes*.

Father Murray's views reflect American constitutional law and tend to identify the Church's teaching with it, yet American constitutional law does not give and does not claim to give a full account of the conception of the dignity of the human person, which, as we have seen, was further developed and enhanced by the council itself and by the magisterium of St. John Paul II and Pope Benedict XVI. Murray's conception of religious freedom as immunity from coercion is not wrong (indeed, one looks at it longingly these days), but again, it must be complemented by a positive view of religious freedom as rooted in the transcendence of human nature.

One of the ways we might celebrate the fiftieth anniversary of DH is to ponder how these differing streams of thought might be more fully integrated.

Reason and Revelation

With that suggestion in mind, I turn to another contribution of DH in the ongoing search for religious freedom, namely, its appeal not only to reason but also to Revelation. And while the second part of DH is entitled "Religious Freedom in the Light of Revelation," let's be clear that the entire declaration is built on the foundation of a harmony between reason and Revelation. That said, the second part offers a largely scriptural account of religious freedom as resting on "a chief tenet of Catholic teaching," viz., "that man's response to God in faith should be voluntary" (DH, no. 10).

The scriptural account does not present religious liberty as a clear and distinct biblical concept. Rather, it arises out of the image of the Savior as "meek and humble of heart": Jesus who listened compassionately to those he encountered along the way; Jesus who showed compassion to erring sinners, yet challenged them to embrace the life-changing truth of the Gospel. Indeed, it was he who said, "The truth will set you free!" Jesus taught us about the weeds and wheat growing together in the field yet warned us that one day we would give an account of our freedom. Jesus acknowledged the legitimacy of civil power, "but he clearly warned that the higher rights of God must be upheld" (DH, no. 11).

Here we can clearly see how DH is both old and new. It rests on the Church's settled teaching regarding the voluntary nature of the act of faith, while within the context of religious freedom teaching us how the Lord draws us to himself so as to evoke from us a free response of love. Here DH invites us to see wholehearted faith in Christ and in his Church as the ultimate fulfillment of the God-given gift of human freedom, though at the same time it does not rule out the religious freedom of those who fail to make an explicit act of faith or any act of faith at all. The document does not see human reason as "self-contained" but rather open to the light of Revelation, just as it does not see human nature as self-contained, with only a fragile nexus that links it to the divine (namely, the nonrepugnance of obediential potency). In our woundedness we are nonetheless open to truth and to God.

DH and the New Evangelization

Because DH allows the light of Revelation and reason to shine on the question of religious liberty, it contributes greatly to the New Evangelization. This theme is struck at the very beginning of the declaration, where it says, "We believe that this one true religion subsists in the Catholic and Apostolic Church, to whom the Lord Jesus committed the task of spreading it among all the people, saying to his apostles, 'Go, therefore, and make disciples of all the nations, baptizing them in the name of the Father, and of the Son, and of the Holy Spirit, teaching them to observe all that I have commanded you'" (DH, no. 1; Mt 28:19–20).

To understand how DH contributes to the New Evangelization, we should take note of what it says about religious liberty as it pertains to individuals and as it pertains to churches, religious communities, and the like.

Because DH anchors religious freedom in human nature, the individual human person is the primary subject of religious freedom. At the same time, DH connects individual and communal religious liberty when it says that the Church herself, as a spiritual authority, must have "as much freedom in action as the care of man's salvation demands" (DH, no. 13). Conversely, individual believers who open their hearts to God "in interior acts that are voluntary and free" have the right to "express these interior acts externally, participating with others in religious matters and professing [their] religion in a communal way" (DH, no. 3). Stating that the religious freedom of the Church is a fundamental principle in the relationship between the Church and the state and in the context of society itself, DH teaches that the Church "claims for herself freedom as a society of men and women who enjoy the right to live in civil society according to the precepts of the Christian faith" (DH, no. 13). So, just as DH points out the obligation of the state to foster and protect the religious liberty of individuals, so too it points out the obligation of the state to foster and protect the religious liberty of the Church.

It should also be said that the dimensions of religious liberty are the same for individuals and communities: both have the right of free inquiry; both have the right to a conscientious search for truth and for God. Both individuals and communities have the right to proclaim their faith within the walls of the Church but also outside of these walls. Both individuals and communities have the right to worship not only at home or within churches but also in public. Further, both individuals and communities have the right and the duty not only to seek the truth but also to hold fast to the truth once known and "to order their whole life in accord with its demands"

(DH, no. 2). For individuals, this certainly extends to conducting one's daily work in accord with the demands of the Gospel. Furthermore, it is not merely a question of obeying the moral law, but even more so a question of bearing witness to the truth. Religious freedom entails the right of individuals to bear witness to their beliefs, not only by word but also in the way they conduct their lives, even when their witness is countercultural. So too religious communities have the right to "govern themselves according to their own norms, honor the Supreme Being with public worship, assist their members in the practice of religious life, strengthen them by instruction, and promote institutions in which members can join together to order their own life according to their religious principles" (DH, no. 4). What's more, religious communities, like individuals, are free to extend their influence into the broader society: "Religious freedom, therefore, should be devoted and ordered to this end, that men and women may come to act with greater responsibility in fulfilling their duties in social life" (DH, no. 8). And finally, the declaration recognizes how religious freedom for both individuals and communities contributes to the common good, for thereby "society itself may enjoy the goods of justice and peace that are born from men's fidelity to God and his holy will" (DH, no. 6).

Let me conclude by mentioning two specific ways in which DH contributes to our understanding of the New Evangelization: first, it contributes to the "content" of the New Evangelization; second, it helps us understand the effects that the New Evangelization should have within the cultures and societies where it is carried out.

With regard to the "content" of the New Evangelization, Pope John Paul II in his first encyclical, *Redemptor Hominis* (RH), deals with DH almost entirely from the point of view of the Church's missionary mandate; he writes, "The Church, because of her divine mission, becomes all the more the guardian of this freedom, which is the condition and basis of the human person's true dignity" (RH, no. 12). As Catholics we are called to respect the religious freedom of every person and to do so precisely because of our obligation to bear witness to the truth. What we proclaim and how we proclaim it should affirm the human dignity of all. The "content" of the New Evangelization must therefore include the transcendent dignity of the human person made in God's image, oriented toward friendship with God and thus bearing in himself a moral obligation to seek the truth that corresponds to the objective natural law, the law written on the heart of man.

Regarding the effect of the New Evangelization upon society, it must be said that, after the right to life, religious freedom, because it pertains to the inmost sanctuary of the human person and his relationship to the very ground of his being, is the first and most fundamental human right, and indeed the source of all the others.[5] When religious freedom is endangered, all human rights are endangered. This is a lesson learned from the oppression of totalitarian regimes, and it is a lesson we must learn as a certain secular orthodoxy overtakes us, an aggressive secularism that is not content simply to live and let live but rather portrays religious freedom as a license to discriminate—and indeed very openly— against people of faith. We can talk all we want about

---

5   See Archbishop William E. Lori, "Life and Freedom: Address to Pro-Life Leaders" (Anaheim, CA, August 6, 2012), http://www. archbalt.org/about-us/the-archbishop/homilies/life-and-freedom.cfm.

forming a just society, but when religious freedom is taken away or when we allow it to evaporate, we are, at the same time, robbing ourselves of the basis for human dignity and setting the stage for a society that is unjust and potentially brutal. Indeed, far from interfering with the public order and the common good, religious freedom is the best friend of the public order and the common good; such freedom is the indispensable ally of true democracy and limited government and the best way to achieve the good of society in accord with the demands of truth. As Fr. Murray himself said, "Freedom is the political method par excellence, whereby the other goals of society are reached."

Indeed, the content and the effects of the New Evangelization are deeply linked. The Good News of salvation unveils the full truth about the human person. What the Church teaches about Christ manifests human dignity in its fullness. Because of this the Church goes forth on her mission with the deepest respect for people in every culture and condition of life, seeking to engage them in a dialogue of truth and love. The Church goes forth on her mission "with deep esteem for 'what is in man'" (RH, no. 12)—never in a spirit of coercion or manipulation, but rather in a way that seeks to build up and strengthen the lives of individuals and society as a whole while looking toward that perfect civilization of truth and love: the reign of God, where Christ is seated at the right hand of the Father.

Thanks for listening! May God bless you, may he bless our Church, and may he bless also these United States of America!

Epilogue

Prayer for the Protection of Religious Liberty

O God our Creator,

from your provident hand we have received
our right to life, liberty, and the pursuit of happiness.
You have called us as your people and given us
the right and the duty to worship you, the only true God,
and your Son, Jesus Christ.
Through the power and working of your Holy Spirit,
you call us to live out our faith in the midst of the world,
bringing the light and the saving truth of the Gospel
to every corner of society.
We ask you to bless us
in our vigilance for the gift of religious liberty.
Give us the strength of mind and heart
to readily defend our freedoms when they are threatened;
give us courage in making our voices heard
on behalf of the rights of your Church

and the freedom of conscience of all people of faith.

Grant, we pray, O heavenly Father,

a clear and united voice to all your sons and daughters

gathered in your Church

in this decisive hour in the history of our nation,

so that, with every trial withstood

and every danger overcome—

for the sake of our children, our grandchildren,

and all who come after us—

this great land will always be "one nation, under God,

indivisible, with liberty and justice for all."

We ask this through Christ our Lord.

Amen.

United States Conference of Catholic Bishops

Suggested Reading

Ecclesiastical Documents

Catechism of the Catholic Church. nos. 2104–2109 (Revised Vatican Edition), Libreria Editrice Vaticana; paperback ISBN: 0385508190.

Compendium of the Social Doctrine of the Church. Libreria Editrice Vaticana; paperback ISBN: 1574556924.

Pope Benedict XVI. "Address of His Holiness Benedict XVI to the Bishops of the United States of America on Their 'Ad Limina' Visit" (January 19, 2012).

Pope Benedict XVI. "Religious Freedom, the Path to Peace: Message for the Celebration of the World Day of Peace" (January 1, 2011).

Second Vatican Council. *Dignitatis Humanae*: Declaration on Religious Freedom (December 7, 1965).

_____. *Nostra Aetate*: Declaration on the Relation of the Church to Non-Christian Religions (October 28, 1965).

Books

Bevans, Stephen B., and Jeffrey Gros. *Evangelization and Religious Freedom*: Ad Gentes *and* Dignitatis Humanae. New York/Mahwah, NJ: Paulist Press, 2009 (see bibliography, 249–251).

Carrillo de Albornoz, A. F. *Religious Liberty*. Translated by John Drury. New York: Sheed and Ward, 1967.

Chaput, Charles J. *Render unto Caesar: Serving the Nation by Living Our Catholic Beliefs in Political Life*. New York: Image, 2009.

George, Robert P. *The Clash of Orthodoxies: Law, Religion, and Morality in Crisis*. Wilmington, DE: ISI Books, 2001.

_____. *Conscience and Its Enemies: Confronting the Dogmas of Liberal Secularism*. Wilmington, DE: ISI Books, 2013.

Grasso, Kenneth, and Robert P. Hunt, eds. *Catholicism and Religious Freedom: Contemporary Reflections on Vatican II's Declaration on Religious Liberty*. Lanham, MD: Rowman and Littlefield, 2006.

McDonagh, Enda. *Freedom or Tolerance: The Declaration on Religious Freedom of Vatican Council II*. Albany, NY: Magi Books, 1967.

Munoz, Vincent Phillip. *Religious Liberty and the American Supreme Court: The Essential Cases and Documents*. Lanham, MD: Rowman and Littlefield, 2015.

Murray, John Courtney. *Religious Liberty: Catholic Struggles with Pluralism*. Edited by J. Leon Hooper. Louisville, KY: Westminster John Knox, 1993.

_____. *We Hold These Truths: Catholic Reflections on the American Proposition*. Lanham, MD: Rowman and Littlefield, 2005.

Religious Liberty: Paul VI and Dignitatis Humanae. *A Symposium Sponsored by the Istituto Paolo VI and the Catholic University of America*. Brescia, Italy: La Nuova Cartografica, 1995.

Rico, Herminio. *John Paul II and the Legacy of* Dignitatis Humanae. Washington, DC: Georgetown University Press, 2002.

Rynne, Xavier. *Vatican Council II*. With a new introduction by the author. Maryknoll, NY: Orbis Books, 1999.

Shah, Timothy Samuel. *Religious Freedom: Why Now? Defending an Embattled Human Right*. Princeton, NJ: Witherspoon Institute, 2012.

Whitehead, Kenneth D., ed. *After 40 Years: Vatican Council II's Diverse Legacy*. South Bend, IN: St. Augustine's Press, 2007.

Yzeermans, Vincent A., ed. *American Participation in the Second Vatican Council*. New York: Sheed and Ward, 1967.

Websites

Acton Institute: Religion and Liberty
http://www.acton.org/pub/religion-liberty

Alliance Defending Freedom
http://www.adflegal.org

American Catholics for Religious Freedom
http://americascatholics.com

American Principles Project
http://americanprinciplesproject.org

Manhattan Declaration
http://manhattandeclaration.org/#0

Religious Freedom Project
http://berkleycenter.georgetown.edu/rfp

The Becket Fund for Religious Liberty
http://www.becketfund.org

The Heritage Foundation, Division on Religion and
Civil Society
http://www.heritage.org/issues/religion-and-civil-
society

Thomas More Law Center
https://www.thomasmore.org

United Nations: Universal Declaration of Human Rights
http://www.un.org/en/documents/udhr/

United States Commission on International Religious
Freedom
http://www.uscirf.gov

United States Conference of Catholic Bishops
http://www.usccb.org/issues-and-action/religious-
liberty/index.cfm

Contact Information

Please contact your members of Congress and urge them to defend religious liberty by opposing the HHS mandate and other attacks on this fundamental right!

You can contact your members of Congress by calling the US Capitol switchboard at (202) 224-3121 or through the websites for the House of Representatives (www.house.gov) and the Senate (www.senate.gov).

To remain involved in this critical struggle and to learn more about issues related to religious liberty, ongoing legal battles, etc., check out these great websites:

US Conference of Catholic Bishops
   http://usccb.org/issues-and-action/religious-liberty/index.cfm

Pennsylvania Catholic Conference
   http://www.pacatholic.org

The Becket Fund for Religious Liberty
   http://www.becketfund.org

Alliance Defending Freedom
   http://www.adflegal.org

About the Contributors

Reverend Dennis J. Billy, CSsR, is scholar-in-residence, professor, and holder of the John Cardinal Krol Chair of Moral Theology at St. Charles Borromeo Seminary, Overbrook.

Most Reverend Charles J. Chaput, OFM Cap., Archbishop of Philadelphia, was a commissioner with the US Commission on International Religious Freedom from 2003 to 2006. His duties included carrying out religious freedom fact-finding missions to China and Turkey and compiling annual reports monitoring global trends in religious liberty. In 2005, he was named a member of the US delegation to Córdoba, Spain, for the "Conference on Anti-Semitism and Other Forms of Intolerance," sponsored by the Organization for Security and Cooperation in Europe. In 2009, the Becket Fund for Religious Liberty awarded him the Canterbury Medal for his work in advancing religious freedom.

Mr. Robert P. George is McCormick Professor of Jurisprudence and Director of the James Madison Program in American Ideals and Institutions at Princeton University. He is the author of *In Defense of Natural Law* (Oxford University Press, 1999) and *Making Men Moral: Civil Liberties and Public Morality* (Oxford University Press, 1993). He has served on the President's Council on Bioethics and as a presidential appointee to the US Commission on Civil Rights. He is a former Judicial Fellow at the Supreme Court of the United States, where he received the Justice Tom C. Clark Award. He is also a recipient of the United States Presidential Citizens Medal and the Honorific Medal for the Defense of Human Rights of the Republic of Poland.

Most Reverend William E. Lori, STD, Archbishop of Baltimore, has held the office of Supreme Chaplain of the Knights of Columbus since 2005. In September 2011 he was appointed as Chair of the newly formed Ad Hoc Committee for Religious Liberty, which was intended to address growing concerns over the erosion of freedom of religion in America.

Mr. William P. Mumma is President and Chairman of the Board of the Becket Fund for Religious Liberty in Washington, DC. He also serves as a trustee at Witherspoon Institute, a board member of the Fellowship of Catholic University Students, and Vice Chairman of the New York Men's Leadership Forum. He has degrees from Georgetown University's School of Foreign Service and Columbia University Business School.

Most Reverend Timothy C. Senior is an Auxiliary Bishop of the Archdiocese of Philadelphia and Rector of St. Charles Borromeo Seminary, Overbrook.

Index

About Leonine Publishers

Leonine Publishers LLC makes fine Catholic literature available to Catholics throughout the English-speaking world. Leonine Publishers offers an innovative "hybrid" approach to book publication that helps authors as well as readers. Please visit our web site at www.leoninepublishers.com to learn more about us. Browse our online bookstore to find more solid Catholic titles to uplift, challenge, and inspire.

Our patron and namesake is Pope Leo XIII, a prudent, yet uncompromising pope during the stormy years at the close of the 19th century. Please join us as we ask his intercession for our family of readers and authors.

Do you have a book inside you? Visit our web site today. Leonine Publishers accepts manuscripts from Catholic authors like you. If your book is selected for publication, you will have an active part in the production process. This book is an example of our growing selection of literature for the busy Catholic reader of the 21st century.

www.leoninepublishers.com

CPSIA information can be obtained at www.ICGtesting.com
Printed in the USA
BVOW05s2323040216

435459BV00001B/2/P